THE AMERICAN THEATER TODAY

THE
AMERICAN
THEATER
TODAY

Edited by ALAN S. DOWNER

BASIC BOOKS, Inc., Publishers
New York *London*

The Authors

EDWARD ALBEE is a producer for Theater 1967 and a playwright whose works include *Zoo Story* (1958), *The Death of Bessie Smith* (1959), *The Sandbox* (1959), *The American Dream* (1960), *Who's Afraid of Virginia Woolf?* (1961), *Tiny Alice* (1964), and *A Delicate Balance* (1966).

RICHARD BARR is a producer for Theater 1967.

ERIC BENTLEY is Brander Matthews Professor of Dramatic Literature at Columbia University. He is the recipient of the George Jean Nathan Award for drama criticism during the 1965–1966 season.

JERRY BOCK is a composer who collaborated with Sheldon Harnick on *The Body Beautiful* (1958), *Fiorello* (1959; Pulitzer Prize, Drama Critics Award, Antoinette Perry Award), *Tenderloin* (1960), *She Loves Me* (1963), and *Fiddler on the Roof* (1964).

ALAN S. DOWNER is Chairman, Department of English, Princeton University.

BERNARD F. DUKORE is Associate Professor of Dramatic Art, Queens College of the City University of New York.

JOHN GASSNER is Sterling Professor of Playwrighting and Dramatic Literature, Yale University.

MALCOLM GOLDSTEIN is Associate Professor of English, Queens College of the City University of New York.

SHELDON HARNICK is a lyricist who has collaborated with Jerry Bock.

BARNARD HEWITT is Professor of Theater Art, University of Illinois, Urbana.

ESTHER M. JACKSON is Professor of Dramatic Arts, Shaw University, Raleigh, North Carolina.

ARTHUR LITHGOW is the Executive Director, McCarter Theatre, Princeton University.

ELLIOT NORTON is the drama critic for the Boston *Record-*

v

American. He is the recipient of the George Jean Nathan Award for drama criticism during the 1963–1964 season.

EDWIN BURR PETTET is Chairman of the School of Dramatic Art, Brandeis University, and Director, Brandeis Theater.

MURRAY SCHISGAL is a playwright whose works include *The Typist and the Tigers* (London 1960; New York 1963), *Ducks and Lovers* (London 1961), *Knit One, Purl One* (Boston 1963), and *Luv* (London 1963; New York, 1964). He is the recipient of the Vernon Rice Award for outstanding achievement in Off-Broadway Theater, 1963.

GERALD WEALES, drama critic for *The Reporter,* is Associate Professor of English, University of Pennsylvania. He is the recipient of the George Jean Nathan Award for drama criticism during the 1964–1965 season.

Preface

In the preparation of this volume, contributions were invited from journalists, critics, historians, and people of the theater itself, both professional and educational. The range of subjects is wide, from the beginnings of American drama to its future, and the range of attitudes varies from description to speculation, from optimism to pessimism. Such width and variety may suggest where the deeper issues and a possible unity lie; primarily they are intended to call attention to the degree to which theater has permeated our culture in all periods and to the elements that have given it a character of its own.

While the first three chapters present an account of the theater in America before World War I the series is not intended as a historical survey. Professor Hewitt, whose *Theatre U.S.A.* is such a survey with full citations of primary accounts, has selected from the period between the War of Independence and the coming of the twentieth century those elements of a dramatic repertory in large part imitative of Europe which reflect the specific interests and attitudes of Americans. Even the major changes in subject matter and technique discussed by John Gassner in his chapter on the New Theater Movement—a movement in which he was an active participant—principally serve to emphasize and develop these elements as distinct from those of the European theaters that gave birth to the "New Theater." Finally, as Professor Goldstein points out, the playwrights of the thirties, a group influenced by the radicalism concomitant with a world-wide depression, were a strong influence in determining the characteristics of the drama after their day, even though their own plays scarcely survived the decade.

Part II focuses on Broadway, for half a century the heart of the American professional theater and, in the years immediately following World War II, a vital, even experimental, production center. Elliot Norton, dean of journalistic reviewers, presents a succinct account of that flourishing period and advances some reasons for its falling off. Eric Bentley looks at comedy, a genre to which the American theater continues to make original contributions. Thornton Wilder, Tennessee Williams, and Arthur Miller, the playwrights from this period most widely produced on the stages of the world, are discussed by three members of the younger generation of academic critics.

In Part III a producer, two playwrights, a lyricist, and a composer of musical comedies discuss their work. Richard Barr has been in the forefront of the effort to discover and develop new talent; Edward Albee and Murray Schisgal have recently made successful jumps from off-Broadway's experimental stages to the frightening responsibilities of Broadway; and Sheldon Harnick and Jerry Bock have refused to rely on formulas in a genre where, more often than not, nothing but formula is expected. It is encouraging that these highly successful representatives of the creative forces in the theater are far from content, are on a restless and determined search for new tools, new techniques. Unlike an older theatrical generation, they are intensely aware of the world beyond the stage door and eager to make artistic contact with it.

Part IV is more speculative. It deals with the most recent forms of what used to be called the "Tributary Theater"—off-Broadway, educational theater, and the growing relationship between professional theater and universities. None of these can be an end in itself; each can enrich the general life of the drama in the future. The scope of the development is indicated by the contributors themselves: Bernard Dukore is a professor of dramatic literature, Edwin Burr Pettet is chairman of the dramatic arts department at a major university, Arthur Lithgow is executive director of a professional repertory company sponsored by a university which provides no formal training in theater art. American institutions of higher learning have assumed greater responsibility for training and apprenticeship in the arts as they have long

viii

done for other professions. While this might lead to formalism, to an insistence on established conventions, the danger is minimal, since the institutions themselves frequently differ in origin, sponsorship, and orientation. What they share is a determination to develop standards but not shackles, a vision but not a preconception for a future repertory to be experienced equally by performers and their audiences. In its affiliation with educational institutions, together with the dispersal of production centers throughout the nation, the theater once again faces the challenge of becoming a positive force in the cultural life of America.

The chapters in this book were originally broadcast over the Voice of America in its *Forum* series.

ALAN S. DOWNER

Princeton, New Jersey
January 1967

Contents

PART I

Background

1 THE AMERICANISM OF AMERICAN THEATER

Barnard Hewitt

American drama did not become completely "American" until about forty years ago, when it attained full maturity in the plays of Eugene O'Neill, Robert Sherwood, Elmer Rice, Sidney Howard, and other playwrights of the 1920's. Nevertheless, almost from the beginning, although American drama was very strongly influenced by European models, particularly British ones, it reflected native American manners and customs, characteristics and ideals, issues and conflicts, as they appeared and developed with our growing country. Most of the early plays have not stood the test of time well enough to warrant revival; American manners, customs, and characteristics have changed so much that they would seem merely quaint and laughable on today's stage. However, some of them are still interesting to read, because they reflect national ideals, significant issues, and major conflicts which helped mold the United States.

Very soon after the Declaration of Independence, when the revolution against Great Britain was only begun, Colonel Robert Munford, a gentleman planter of Virginia, wrote a comedy called *The Patriots* in which he contrasted the genuine patriotism and courage of Meanwell and Trueman with the empty boastfulness of Captain Flash and the ignorant, stupid, self-seeking chauvinism of Thunderbolt, Squib, Colonel Strut, Brazen, and Skip, members of the Committee of Safety, which had set itself to nose out and punish all adherents to Britain. In *The Patriots*, suspected loyalists are haled before the Committee of Safety in hearings which are all too reminiscent of those by the House Un-American Activities Committee in the period of Joseph McCarthy.

Citizens of a new nation, born of a bloody revolution against foreign tyranny, naturally needed to assert an ardent patriotism and love of liberty. This was the theme of many of our early plays, for example, John Burk's *The Battle of Bunker's Hill*, first produced, appropriately enough, in Boston in 1797, and frequently revived for years afterward on the Fourth of July, Independence Day. This crude piece presented little but turgid oratory on the theme of heroic rebellion against mean oppression and outrageous tyranny, and there is one battle scene in which red-coated British professional soldiers stormed the famous hill defended by the motley force of amateur American rebels.

A better and more engaging play expressed the new loyalties in a very different mood. On April 17, 1787, while the Constitutional Convention was still struggling to reconcile sectional rights with necessary federal powers, in a document which would weld the thirteen loosely confederated states into the United States of America, a comedy entitled *The Contrast* by native playwright Royall Tyler was produced at the John Street Theatre in New York. Tyler was young and had seen action in the Revolutionary War. He addressed his audience in a prologue which begins:

> Exult each patriot heart!—this night is shown
> A piece which we may fairly call our own.

The setting of his play is New York City in 1787, and the "contrast" of its title is the contrast between foreign sham and native honesty, between imported vice and home-grown virtue. The hero is Colonel Manly, who has come to the city in his plain country clothes and old army overcoat in order to get onto the pension rolls some of the men who had fought under him in the Revolution. The villain is Dimple, a native New Yorker and a lover of all things British. He is beribboned, bepowdered, and bewigged. He is a fop and an unprincipled rake. Jessamy, his

4

servant, is a vulgar imitation of his master. The Colonel's man, Jonathan, although he is devoted to Manly, proudly rejects the appellation "servant" and calls himself a "true born Yankee son of liberty." Jonathan, like Manly, is from the country. He is illiterate and naïve, but he is shrewd, good-humored, loyal, honest, patriotic and, above all, independent. He was so popular with audiences that he reappeared in many later plays, with different accents, all of them rural.

Fervent patriotism, excessive sensitiveness to criticism from without, and militant flag-waving are of course an aspect of nationalism, which is always very strong in a young nation. A young nation, like an adolescent child, apparently has to assert its identity in order to discover it.

Internationalism is often thought of as a relatively new attitude in America, dating perhaps from World War I. That it was present very early is evident from William Dunlap's blank-verse tragedy *André*, which was produced at the Park Theatre in New York in 1798. Dunlap based his drama on an actual episode of the Revolution. John André, a major in the British army, had been caught in civilian clothes behind the American lines, where he had been sent to arrange for the betrayal of West Point by General Benedict Arnold. André had been tried by a military court, condemned as a spy, and hanged on October 2, 1780. The plot of Dunlap's play consists of a series of futile attempts to obtain from General Washington a pardon or a stay of execution for André. André was not a professional spy but an officer and a gentleman, and there were other extenuating circumstances. However, Washington puts the cause of liberty above personal feelings, and history takes its course—but not before a young American officer friend of André has torn the black cockade from his hat and flung it to the ground in youthful rebellion against authority. On opening night, this brought hisses from the audience and pressure for the play to be withdrawn. Moreover, in one of the quiet scenes, two American officers while away the tedium of night guard duty by debating at some length whether a strong United

5

States can be better built independent of "entangling alliances" with European countries or by renewing and strengthening ties with Britain and the Continent of Europe.

As the Revolutionary War receded farther into the past, the theme of heroic rebellion against tyranny and oppression appeared in our drama in new guises. In 1829, John Augustus Stone's *Metamora, or The Last of the Wampanoags,* written especially for Edwin Forrest, America's first native-born star tragedian, had its première. The play was laid not in the immediate past but in the earlier period when the first white settlers were driving the original Americans from the lands east of the Allegheny Mountains. The hero is not, as one might expect, the leader of the whites, but the leader of the Indians, Chief Metamora. Metamora is an American version of Rousseau's Noble Savage. He is filled with love for his people and for his wife and with magnificent scorn for the cruel, treacherous whites. He resists the invaders with superhuman stoicism, strength, and courage until, with all hope gone, he slays his wife to save her from the enemy and dies from bullet wounds inflicted by the ruthless foe. The play, paradoxically, appears to express both the love of liberty and the guilt of the conqueror, both pride in the strength and determination which were rapidly winning the lands west of the Alleghenies and sympathy for the victims of that new victory.

The West was won by a new American type, the frontiersman, who combined traits of the Indian and the Yankee with some entirely his own. One of his first appearances on the stage was in James K. Paulding's comedy *The Lion of the West,* written in 1831 for the actor James H. Hackett. The title role, that of Nimrod Wildfire, is a thinly disguised portrait of the real Davy Crockett, who in 1831 was not only still very much alive but also very much in the public eye as the congressman from Kentucky. Wildfire, not unlike Colonel Manly in *The Contrast,* is contrasted with a caddish Englishman who attempts to pass himself off as a lord. But Wildfire is very different from the quiet, modest, gentlemanly Manly. He writes to his Uncle Freeman in New York:

"Let all the fellers there know—I'm half horse, half Alligator, a touch of the airth-quake, with a sprinkling of steamboat." But, as Freeman assures his wife, and as events show: ". . . All this whimsical extravagance of speech results from mere exuberance of spirits, and his total ignorance of conventional restraint he overbalances by a heart which would scorn to do a mean or a dishonest action."

The Lion of the West was revised two years later to capitalize on the notoriety of a book with the condescending title *Domestic Manners of the Americans,* published in 1832 by an English-woman, Frances M. Trollope. Mrs. Trollope had lived for some time in Cincinnati and visited the larger cities of the East. She was shocked by many of the crudities of life in the new country, by the almost universal chewing and spitting of tobacco, by the informal dress and behavior in public places, and by the lack of subservience in servants. Paulding's play was altered to make room for a visiting Englishwoman named Mrs. Wallop, who discovers new and wonderful crudities in Nimrod Wildfire, but who also discovers eventually that beneath that barbarous outside there beats a warm and honest heart.

While America was growing geographically through the winning of the West, it was growing in wealth and population in the cities of the East. And those cities were producing a life as crude and colorful as the backwoods of Kentucky had a few years before. In 1848, another forgotten play, *A Glance at New York,* introduced Nimrod Wildfire's urban counterpart in the character of Mose the Bowery Bhoy, who loved to run with the engine of his volunteer fire company and enjoyed nothing better than a good knockdown, drag-out fight with rival fire-fighters. Like Wildfire, he was illiterate, ignorant, and boastful; like Wildfire and Jonathan, he was shrewd, honest, and narrowly patriotic. Like Wildfire, Jonathan, and Metamora, he was as independent as a hog on ice. And under his red shirt there beat a warm and honest heart.

The great theme of love of liberty and rebellion against tyranny appeared not only in plays set in America, like *Bunker's Hill* and

Metamora, but also in plays set in foreign lands. Robert Montgomery Bird's tragedy *The Gladiator,* which, like *Metamora,* was written for Edwin Forrest, deals with the revolt led by Spartacus, a gladiatorial slave, against the rulers of Rome in 73 B.C. It was popular in 1831 when it was first played because the revolt of the Roman gladiators was equated with that of the American colonists. Fifteen years later Walt Whitman could say with reason that *The Gladiator* was about as full of abolitionism as an egg is of meat. Indeed, throughout the first act Spartacus eloquently expresses his rebellion against slavery and pleads with his master, Lentulus, to buy his wife and son so that they may be reunited. At the time of Whitman's statement, Spartacus could more easily have been identified with the oppressed American Negro of 1846 than with the oppressed American white of 1776.

The appearance in our drama of rural Jonathan, Western Wildfire, and urban Mose were signs of sectionalism. Increasing tension over Negro slavery was promoting sectionalism in a more virulent form, and this too soon found expression in drama. Some plays exploited the conflict between North and South for sensational melodrama and soothing sentiment. One of these was *The Octoroon* by Dion Boucicault. Boucicault had been born in Ireland and educated in England, but much of his life as actor and playwright was spent in America, and *The Octoroon* is set on a plantation in Louisiana. It represents the slaves as lovable children devoted to their benevolent masters, and it carefully skirts the incendiary question of abolition. But there were also the dramatizations of Harriet Beecher Stowe's *Uncle Tom's Cabin,* which, though they made the most of the novel's melodrama and sentiment, still retained its crusading spirit.

When the first of these dramatizations was produced in New York in 1852, a New York *Herald* editorial asked: "What will our Southern friends think of all our professions of respect for their delicate social institution of slavery, when they find that our amusements are overdrawn caricatures exhibiting our hatred against it and against them?" And it advised "all concerned to drop the play" which is "calculated . . . to become a firebrand

8

of the most dangerous character to the peace of the whole country."

The Negro had appeared earlier in American drama, but only as a comic plantation hand or house servant. In *Uncle Tom's Cabin,* George Harris, a slave, but educated, talented, ambitious, and determined to be free or die in the attempt, is the hero of the first half, and Uncle Tom, simple, honest, loyal, and done to death by the malevolent Legree, is the hero of the second half.

Actors and managers ignored the *Herald*'s prudent advice, and the play *Uncle Tom's Cabin,* like the novel, helped to spread the flames of conflict, until the South's "delicate social institution" was consumed in the conflagration of civil war. Because slavery was confined to the Southern states, the conflict appeared to be primarily a sectional conflict, a conflict between the industrial North and the agrarian South. But Negro slavery was profitable to a great many people in the North as well as in the South, and when the chips were down a good many Northerners opposed the war. There were anti-draft riots in New York, and many Copperheads, as the Northern sympathizers were called, did their best to sabotage the Union cause. Thus the conflict was more than a sectional conflict; it was a general conflict between materialism and idealism, between the desire to hang on to wealth and power and concern for human rights and human dignity. *Uncle Tom's Cabin* left no doubt on which side in that conflict lay the right.

The Civil War itself was reflected in American drama, but, as if the realities of that bitter and destructive struggle were too dreadful to be faced, it was reflected very largely in plays which mirrored the wish to heal the wounds of war and to forget its horrors. Bronson Howard's very popular play *Shenandoah* used General Sheridan's famous ride and other events of the war primarily to produce tension and pathos and to complicate the romance of four pairs of lovers. And William Gillette's *Secret Service* used the siege of Richmond to generate the suspense necessary to a drama of spies and counterspies.

However, James A. Herne's *The Reverend Griffith Davenport* came to grips with the Civil War's great issues. Griffith Davenport is a Virginia gentleman who has inherited a plantation, and with it Negro slaves, but he is also an ordained Methodist minister, convinced that slavery is morally wrong. In spite of the opposition of his wife and son, and even of the slaves themselves, for whom as free men there will be no place in Virginia, he sets his slaves free. To escape harassment by his neighbors, he flees to Washington, D.C., to await the outcome of the war. There Abraham Lincoln calls upon him to guide Federal troops invading his native state. Loyalty to the Union triumphs over loyalty to Virginia; Davenport helps Lincoln save the nation.

The love of individual liberty, which was a big factor in the abolition of slavery, and the urge for greater material prosperity, which brought wave after wave of immigrants from Europe, continued to build the country geographically, pushing the frontier west until it lay on the shores of the Pacific. Individual liberty in the form of free enterprise in business continued to build the industrial cities of the East and the railroads which soon tamed the Wild West.

By 1874, when Frank H. Murdoch's *Davy Crockett* was first performed, the United States had grown so large, so strong, and so self-confident that it no longer felt the need to assert its superiority to the countries of Europe. Its theme was no longer the contrast between the American and the European but between the Western American and the Eastern American. Murdoch's play owed considerably more to the poem "Young Lochinvar" by the foreigner Walter Scott than it did to the historical exploits of the American Davy Crockett. Murdoch's frontiersman is strong to bar the cabin door with his right arm against the ravening wolves and to carry off the lovely heroine, when he learns that she is being forced into marriage with a weakling from the decadent East. But he is no Nimrod Wildfire, uncouth and boastful, half horse, half alligator. This Davy Crockett is modest and unassuming. He not only has a warm and honest heart, he has the manners of a true gentleman as well. He is Nature's nobleman: the new, free, vital American, product of the West's wide-open spaces.

But if the West occasionally produced a natural nobleman, it produced a good many plain, ordinary, hard-working ranchers and miners. And it produced more than a few outlaws and desperados, who displayed their individualism by preying on ordinary citizens. In the absence of effective government, ordinary citizens took the law into their own hands. Lynch law was also a product of the West.

William Vaughn Moody saw some of the complexities of the conflict between West and East, and expressed them in a play called *The Great Divide*. In it, Ruth Jordan, a gently reared and cultivated young woman from New England, who is betrothed to an Easterner, is left unprotected on a ranch in Arizona. Three Western desperados break in and threaten her with rape. She offers to marry the least repulsive of them, if he will protect her from the others. Stephen Ghent accepts the proposition. He buys off one of his companions, kills the other in equal combat, and claims his prize. The second act finds the ill-matched couple married and settled in mining country. They have an infant son, and Ghent is working hard and successfully to support his family. However, Ruth's pride and her puritanical sense of guilt, which tells her she has sold herself, prevent her from seeing that Ghent has changed, that he is no longer the desperado who broke into the Arizona ranch house. So she runs away to New England to bring up her son in what seems to her a respectable atmosphere. But she can no longer be happy in the East, and when Ghent seeks her out, she is persuaded to see that her puritanism is wrong, stultifying and life-denying, that the way of life lies with her husband, who stands revealed as no longer the rootless, unprincipled outlaw, but as the good strong, free, new citizen of the West. The great divide no longer separates them. They are united in a new life which will combine the best of both East and West.

The United States was settled and developed very largely by immigrants from Europe seeking religious and political freedom and the opportunity to improve their economic position. Throughout the nineteenth century this country offered golden opportunity for material advancement. The combination of ap-

11

parently unlimited natural resources and almost complete freedom from government interference brought particularly rapid
growth between 1870 and 1900, but it brought feverish speculation, ruthless exploitation, and shameful waste and corruption as
well. In 1873, *The Gilded Age,* a dramatization of the novel by
Mark Twain and Charles Dudley Warner, focused on Colonel
Sellers, who is full of madly glorious schemes for making untold
millions overnight and has the gift of gab to beguile the gullible.
Sellers is a fast and plausible talker, but he is essentially warm-
hearted and charitable and his schemes are so far removed from
reality that they hurt nobody but himself and his long-suffering
family. But around the self-deceiving Sellers swarm the canny
ones: the Wall Street bankers and brokers; unprincipled promoters of very realistic schemes to make very definite millions
quickly by the exploitation of land, water, minerals, and their
fellow citizens. And around the bankers and brokers hang the
venal state governors and federal congressmen, whose palms must
be greased so that the promoters may reap the harvest. Each one is
irresistibly impelled to fill his own pockets, no matter what the
cost to others. Against these vultures are set the engineers, the
architects, the surveyors, the honest, hard-working, farsighted
Americans who do the solid building and are content with a rea-
sonable wage and the satisfaction of genuine accomplishment.

Bronson Howard's *The Henrietta* in 1887 presented the evils of
large-scale speculation as they affected the Wall Street operator
and his immediate family and friends. Old Nick Vanalstyne is the
master manipulator of the stock market, a Jay Gould for whom
speculation is an exciting game to be played to win, regardless of
the means employed. For his son, Nicholas, Jr., it is more like a
disease, one which drives him to ruin his father and to kill himself. Almost everyone in the play is infected with the itch for un-
earned riches. Even Dr. Murray Hilton, rector of a fashionable
church, preaches against materialism on Sunday and on Monday
morning is in Vanalstyne's office hoping to pick up a tip that will
enable him to make a killing in the stock market.

Today the conflict between materialism and idealism takes different forms from those it assumed in the nineteenth century, but it is no less acute. We are proud of our industrial strength, of our prosperity, of our affluent society, but we are plagued by the problem of the apparently permanently unemployed. Although many of our young people crowd our schools and colleges preparing themselves for monetarily rewarding jobs in business and industry, some instead join the Peace Corps to help the less unfortunate in other countries and still others enlist in the voter-registration drive in Mississippi to help the less fortunate here at home.

The struggle for individual liberty is far from over; indeed, it is apparent in the movement to secure civil rights for Negro citizens. As in 1860, it has opened the breach between North and South, and renewed the conflict between state and federal sovereignty. In a number of states, the states' rights doctrine is being proclaimed again in angry protest against the recent Supreme Court decision which requires reapportionment of state legislatures and other elective bodies strictly on the basis of population, in order for the first time to give the city dweller's vote the same weight as the farmer's.

Although big business is now spread across the length and breadth of the land and the frontier no longer exists, Eastern bankers and Eastern money are still bogeymen with which to scare Western voters in national elections. And although federal agencies and federal money provide indispensable services in every state of the Union, the powers of the federal government are still an issue and both major political parties declare that federal spending should be curtailed.

Old-style flag-waving patriotism and narrow nationalism are every day more and more anachronistic in a world knit irrevocably together by jet planes and Telstar communication, but some Americans still yearn for the old comfortable isolation.

The forces and the conflicts, which are reflected in early American drama, are the forces, the issues, and the conflicts which molded America, which made the country what it is today. And although they have taken on new forms, those forces have not yet disappeared, those conflicts have not yet been resolved. Today's Americanism is foreshadowed in the Americanism of yesterday's American drama.

2 PIONEERS OF THE NEW THEATER MOVEMENT

John Gassner

The story of the Provincetown and the Washington Square Players and other pioneering groups between 1915 and 1929 holds great interest for anyone who wants to observe the American theater in a proper perspective. To do this, one must consider the efforts of these groups both as a native development and as an extension of the European stage.

On the surface, the story is simple enough. In 1915, while Europe was embroiled in World War I, several noteworthy efforts to orient the American stage toward modern art occurred almost simultaneously in New York City. One theatrical group, the Neighborhood Playhouse, was an outgrowth of a wealthy family's interest in social welfare. This little theater was located in the Lower East Side section of Manhattan, where an economically deprived immigrant population stood midway between the Old World and the New. That a good deal of talent should have been discovered in this colorful milieu is not surprising; and that the stage productions should have reflected an interest in the folklore and folk art of other nations was inevitable. The Neighborhood Playhouse was indeed most celebrated for its experiments in the art of the dance and for tasteful musical entertainment. It attained its greatest popular success with *The Grand Street Follies*, a gay revue consisting of brilliantly conceived sketches, such as a satire on the expressionist use of step platforms, or so-called *Jessnertreppen*.

The artistic niveau of the Neighborhood Playhouse was attained in two major productions featuring East European and Oriental stylization. One was the first professional production of S. A. Ansky's folk play *The Dybbuk,* in English, shortly after its famous Habima Theatre production in Hebrew; the other was the colorful Hindu classic *The Little Clay Cart.* Up to the end of its career in 1927, the Neighborhood Playhouse management continued to favor the art of dramatic stylization at which the company excelled. It experimented with equal determination, though with less success, whether it presented Lorca's poetic drama *Blood Wedding,* an obscure symbolist play by William Butler Yeats, or a witty eighteenth-century literary satire such as Sheridan's *The Critic.*

Its contribution to the American theater of the period from 1915 to 1927 was nevertheless limited by this very penchant for stylization and artistic refinement. It remained for the Washington Square Players and the Provincetown Players to infiltrate the professional theater in America, and to affect it profoundly. The main current of modernization was *not* exotic.

The slightly older of the two groups, the Washington Square Players, was formally established in 1914. It presented its first productions the following year, in midtown Manhattan in a small theater called the Bandbox. The group consisted of intellectuals, social rebels, and artists. One of the leaders was the scene designer Lee Simonson, who was steeped in European avant-garde movements and helped to revolutionize American scenic art. He advanced the cause of expressionism, for example, when he later staged Ernst Toller's *Masse Mensch (Man and the Masses)* and designed the scenery for Elmer Rice's *The Adding Machine,* a noteworthy satire on the depersonalization of man in modern society. The ruling spirit of the organization was the British-born Lawrence Langner, who combined playwriting with the successful practice of patent law. His associate, Philip Moeller, was a successful Broadway playwright when he joined the organization. He soon became an outstanding director of such unusual plays as O'Neill's *Strange Interlude* and *Mourning Becomes Electra.* Some of the ablest actors of the next decade also joined the Washington Square Players; among them were the soon to become famous Helen Westley, Katharine Cornell, and Roland Young. Also associated with them, though more loosely, were such idealists of social reform as the Socialist leader Rose Pastor Stokes and the journalist John Reed, the author of *Ten Days That Shook the World*, who died of typhus while covering the Russian Revolution.

The Washington Square Players revealed a characteristic partiality for one-act plays that expressed sophisticated views on sex, such as *Helena's Husband* by Philip Moeller and Alice Gerstenberg's once very popular Freudian fantasy *Overtones*. Later, the young company went beyond fashionable intellectualism and enriched its one-act repertory with effectively realistic productions. These included O'Neill's early sea play *In the Zone*. But the ambitions of this theatrical group, which brought it to the precincts of the Broadway professional theater, reached out rapidly to the production of full-length drama.

By the spring of 1916 the young company attempted to stage a poetic drama by Maeterlinck and followed this with a production of Chekhov's *The Sea Gull*. And in 1917 it plunged deeper into atmospheric drama with Leonid Andreyev's allegory *The Life of Man*, in which Andreyev's ill-fated nameless hero is accompanied throughout life by a personification of Death. During the same season, the struggling amateurs undertook to present Ibsen's *Ghosts*, which was still regarded as vaguely avant-garde and faintly scandalous in the United States. And disregarding an early ban, the little group of rebels also produced Bernard Shaw's *Mrs. Warren's Profession*.

Without ever achieving popular success, the Washington Square Players managed to present a total of sixty-two one-act and six full-length plays in New York during a brief career, which came to a close in May 1918 while America was involved in World War I. However, it was characteristic of this spirited group that it reassembled soon after the cessation of hostilities. It re-established itself as a producing company, this time, hopefully, in the professional theater, and started gathering around it a growing number

17

of subscribers. Calling itself the Theatre Guild, the reconstructed group forged ahead to become America's outstanding producing company, usually presenting six carefully produced plays each theatrical season.

With the success of this enterprise, first in New York and later also in a number of other large cities in which the Theatre Guild had a subscription audience, the American theater won international prestige. Other managements had equal or greater success with some individual presentations, but none had a comparable record of consistently distinguished productions year after year. This was the case even when the Theatre Guild, like other managements, suffered serious reverses from the economic depression of the 1930's, World War II, and the subsequent inflation of the costs of theatrical production. For nearly a decade, during the period of the Depression, the Theatre Guild seemed to be overshadowed by its own offshoot, the Group Theatre, which specialized in dramas of direct or indirect social conflict. But the parent organization possessed a resilience that enabled it to outlast its offspring by more than two decades.

The Theatre Guild was attuned to the important task of providing the American theater with the broadest possible links with the European stage. This was evident in several ways. The Theatre Guild became Bernard Shaw's official producer in the United States and accounted for a number of his world premières. It also gave productions of such imaginative works of the first quarter of the twentieth century as Ferenc Molnár's *Liliom,* Karel Čapek's fantastic *R.U.R.,* Ernst Toller's *Masse Mensch,* Georg Kaiser's *From Morn to Midnight,* and Franz Werfel's *The Goat Song.* There was a time when, under the present writer's administration of the Theatre Guild's play department, direct links were maintained with the theater in Britain, France, Italy, Germany, Austria, Hungary, and Russia. Later, the Theatre Guild, despite its interest in European drama, increasingly drew upon the work of American authors. It presented some of the outstanding plays of Eugene O'Neill, Elmer Rice, Robert Sherwood, Maxwell Anderson, and Philip Barry, whose work was influenced by European dramatic art but was distinctly American in style and idiom. The Theatre Guild also produced outstanding American contributions to the musical stage, including the renowned *Porgy and Bess,* later widely toured in European capitals. Thus, out of the Washington Square Players venture, which lasted less than four years, came a substantial part of the stimulus that modernized the American stage and soon enabled it to make its own contributions to the world of modern theater.

In the mind of historically oriented critics, however, it is the third of the New York groups, the Provincetown Players, that stands out as the most important. It maintained amateur, or semi-amateur, status virtually to the end of its career in 1929, whereas the original Washington Square Players disbanded in 1918. Moreover, the Provincetown Players was primarily interested in producing the work of new American playwrights; and it rapidly attained prominence with O'Neill's most advanced experiments in dramatic style. Although the leading American designer, Robert Edmond Jones, was closely associated with it, the Provincetown company came to be regarded as essentially a "playwrights' theater." It was chiefly modern playwriting that still needed to be developed in the United States, and it was at this task that the Provincetown excelled.

Characteristically, the Provincetown group started presenting plays informally in an artists' colony—namely, Provincetown, on Cape Cod. The first two plays, given during the summer of 1915, were shown first in a private home and then repeated in a deserted old house on a wharf. A suitable audience of intellectuals and artists lent support to the project. The better known of the two little plays was written by Susan Glaspell and her husband, George Cram Cook. Entitled *Suppressed Desires,* the play was a genial satire on the vogue of psychoanalysis, then in its infancy in the United States. A second bill of one-act plays was presented during the same summer at the "Wharf Theatre," as this little theater came to be called. One of these was Cook's *Change Your Styles,* a comedy about life among artists. The other play, called *Contemporaries,* was the work of the short-story writer Wilbur Daniel Steele. It attracted audiences with an appeal for social justice. It was based upon the well-publicized case of a young idealist who had tried to provide shelter for some homeless unemployed men by leading them into a church and received a prison sentence for his efforts.

The group returned to the Provincetown wharf for a second season in 1916, and with augmented forces. One of the new members was the young Eugene O'Neill. The first bill included a revival of *Suppressed Desires* and a new play of social protest by the young Harvard-educated journalist John Reed. Three additional productions were given in that season. The first of these was O'Neill's moving one-act sea play *Bound East for Cardiff.* It became the outstanding production of the summer, although Susan Glaspell also won considerable success with a powerful short farm tragedy called *Trifles.* Encouraged by success in Provincetown, the young artists proceeded to establish a theater in New York's bohemian Greenwich Village in a tiny building seating 150 spectators.

Subscriptions multiplied, and the company acquired talented new members. Famous and soon to become famous writers and artists provided the plays and performed in them. Especially noteworthy were the new one-act plays contributed by O'Neill to the first two New York seasons. Among them were the little sea plays *'Ile* and *The Long Voyage Home.* Other new one-act plays were supplied by Susan Glaspell, the novelist Floyd Dell, and the poets Alfred Kreymborg, James Oppenheim, and Maxwell Bodenheim. They were joined during the season of 1918–19 at slightly more ample new quarters, in a converted stable at 133 MacDougal Street, by the outstanding woman poet of the period, Edna St. Vincent Millay, who acted as well as wrote for the company.

The first season in their new home included O'Neill's atmospheric *The Moon of the Caribees,* and the next season was made noteworthy by Edna St. Vincent Millay's *commedia dell'arte* masterpiece *Aria da Capo.* Soon the Provincetown Players acquired a succession of longer works, O'Neill's *The Emperor Jones* and *Diff'rnt* and Susan Glaspell's *Inheritors*. The 1921–2 season included a long play by Theodore Dreiser, *The Hand of the Potter*, the novelist's only stage production. The season also had O'Neill's famous expressionist drama *The Hairy Ape*, in which the physically impressive actor Louis Wolheim played the central role of a tragically bewildered stoker who stands, actually and symbolically, midway between humanity and the animal world. In the season of 1923–4, the Provincetown Players gave unwonted attention to the European drama with productions of August Strindberg's *The Spook* (or *Ghost*) *Sonata* and Molière's comedy *Georges Dandin, ou Le Mari Confondu* in a translation by the distinguished American critic Stark Young. But they also revived *The Emperor Jones,* with the young actor-singer Paul Robeson in the principal part, and presented an impressive new play by O'Neill, *All God's Chillun Got Wings,* a tragedy of miscegenation. Here Paul Robeson starred in the role of the Negro law student Jim Harris, who marries a fallen white girl out of compassion only to be emotionally drained by her mad desire to pull him down to her own level.

After this memorable season, the Provincetown Players reached another peak of creativity with a moving presentation of four of O'Neill's best one-act plays under the collective title of *S.S. Glencairn,* as well as a sparkling production of a Gilbert and Sullivan operetta, *Patience.* With a remarkable outpouring of energy, the company also presented the German playwright Walter Hasenclever's fantasy *Beyond* and the French playwright Charles Vildrac's *Michel Auclair,* as well as a lively American folk comedy, *Ruint,* by Hatcher Hughes. By then, moreover, the Provincetown company was also producing plays in the more commodious quarters of the Greenwich Village Theatre. Although the first production there, Stark Young's *The Saint,* proved unsuccessful, the second production was O'Neill's most distinguished early drama, *Desire under the Elms,* a naturalistic tragedy of extraordinary power. It was staged and designed by Robert Edmond Jones. The famous actor Walter Huston played the important role of a

21

New England farmer betrayed by his new young wife and his morbidly hostile youngest son by a previous marriage.

In the 1925–6 season at the Provincetown Playhouse the productions declined in effectiveness, but the company's presentation of Strindberg's *A Dream Play* for the first time in New York was worth noting, and a streamlined production of Gluck's operatic masterpiece *Orpheus and Eurydice* was altogether admirable despite the smallness of the stage. The season also had a good revival of *The Emperor Jones* when Charles Gilpin returned to his original role as the West Indian dictator trapped in the jungle by atavistic fears. In 1926–7 only one production made a strong impression, but this one introduced an important new American playwright, Paul Green, whose sympathetic drama of Negro life, *In Abraham's Bosom,* won the coveted Pulitzer Prize in 1927. A venture in theatrical stylization with Carlo Goldoni's *Princess Turandot,* while unsuccessful, was noteworthy as an attempt to reproduce the historically important Russian production by Stanislavsky's most famous pupil, Eugene Vakhtangov. The 1927–8 season was also disappointing, but it contained the poet E. E. Cummings' imaginative avant-garde satire *him.*

The group's final season of 1928–9 presented productions both at the downtown Provincetown Playhouse and at the "uptown" Garrick Theatre. Nothing, however, could prevent the dissolution of the Provincetown Players by then, and the economic depression that started in 1929 claimed one more victim.

With the demise of the Provincetown Players we come to the end of an important phase of the American theater. The brief account I have given of the Provincetown's major productions by no means exhausts the historical interest of this company's enterprise. It does not do justice to the many talented people who joined the Provincetown Players at one time or another to direct and design the plays or to play in them. But, appropriately, the Provincetown ended its career, just as it began it, with the work of a new American playwright, Virgil Geddes' bleak Midwestern farm tragedy *The Earth Between.* The Provincetown remained a "playwrights' " theater to the very end.

To obtain an even larger perspective on the Provincetown and its sister groups it would be necessary to take note of other production activities in New York. Among these was the independent partnership of Kenneth Macgowan, Robert Edmond Jones, and O'Neill at the Greenwich Village Theatre for several years. It was there that they produced Edmond Rostand's imaginative last play *The Last Night of Don Juan* and O'Neill's highly experimental mask-drama *The Great God Brown,* subsequently transferred to Broadway.

A second noteworthy venture was the progressive Actors Theatre, founded in 1922, which sustained itself on Broadway for three stimulating seasons. It put on excellent Ibsen and Shaw productions as well as symbolist and expressionist plays by other writers. We must also take note of an effort to establish a second playwrights' theater, called the New Playwrights Company, which received financial assistance for several seasons from the philanthropist and art-lover Otto Kahn. By the time the New Playwrights Company ended its brief career in 1927, it had produced provocative, although consistently unsuccessful, plays by such insurgent authors as John Dos Passos, Upton Sinclair, John Howard Lawson, Paul Sifton, and Michael Gold.

These attempts to create a vital modern theater in the United States were, moreover, part of a widespread movement to establish experimental little theaters in other large cities, such as Chicago, Boston, Cleveland, and Detroit. And in such smaller communities as Chapel Hill (North Carolina) and Charleston (South Carolina) regional material was developed into vivid folk plays by a number of young writers, including Thomas Wolfe, Du Bose Heyward, and Paul Green. Even before the establishment of the Provincetown Players, as early as 1912, the so-called "little theaters" devoted themselves to producing plays without regard for the practical considerations of the commercial theater. Before long, moreover, even the commercial theater began to reflect the interest in experimentation fostered by the leaders of the little theaters as well as, of course, by their European predecessors, among whom Strindberg was perhaps the most influential playwright. O'Neill observed this in a program note for the Provincetown Players in 1924 when he wrote that "in creating a modern theatre . . . it is the most apt symbol of our good intentions that we start with a play by August Strindberg, for Strindberg was the precursor of all modernity in our present theatre. . . ."

It is essential to observe, finally, that no single style of theater dominated the "little theater" movement. It was *eclectic* rather than dogmatic, so that naturalistic and poetic aims were often pursued by the same authors and producing companies. Even from our necessarily rapid review, it is abundantly evident that a vast curiosity about life and art and a remarkable willingness to conduct experiments in a variety of styles characterized the movement. And, as is well known, this tendency was most vividly exemplified by the career of the American avant-garde's chief discovery, Eugene O'Neill.

3 THE PLAYWRIGHTS OF THE 1930'S

Malcolm Goldstein

For Americans as well as for Europeans, to review the events of the 1930's is to recall a period of relentless strain. Beginning in unprecedented economic dislocation and ending in global war, the decade was a massive trial of endurance. Yet in America it was also a time of hope. Encouraged by President Roosevelt's assertion that fear was the greatest enemy, the nation held to its democratic principles and gradually regained the strength of which it had so suddenly been deprived in the last months of 1929. In the main, the literature of the period, though always mindful of unemployment and militarism, reflected the optimism of the people. The response of the theater to the appeal for forthright action to relieve economic pressure and the threat of war was commendably strong; then, as now, intellectual playwrights were scarce, but they were present in sufficient numbers to create exhilarating drama. Social protest was in the air; it was the dominant direction of creative thought. Each new theatrical season brought a fresh supply of dramatized injunctions against materialism and injustice. The general result, despite the usual, expected spate of tractlike propaganda pieces, was a praiseworthy drama which prodded the conscience and stimulated the imagination.

Understandably, older writers—those who had had their first successes in or before the 1920's—reacted somewhat more slowly to new drifts of thought than the writers who arrived in the theater after the beginning of the Depression. With few notable ex-

25

ceptions, veteran playwrights were not inclined to look with favor on drastic changes in the American social order and political system. They were continuing in their chosen field and commenting on the world around them from positions which they had long held, unlike the young writers who were sparked to create drama out of distress over contemporary conditions. Three older playwrights, Maxwell Anderson, S. N. Behrman, and Robert E. Sherwood, exemplify the best expression of the traditional middle-class attitude of Broadway. That is not to say, however, that they represent the total Broadway scene of the 1930's; not only were their social attitudes different from those of many other writers of their generation, but their competence raised them above the level of most. As to their attitudes, what is most readily discernible is their reluctance to give up the values of the past, even as they struggle to understand the present. Yet all were men of good will to whom, increasingly, the contemporary uneasiness became a matter for grave concern.

During the decade, Maxwell Anderson wrote plays of many sorts—tragedy, comedy with and without music, and melodrama —but in only one play, *Both Your Houses,* did he catch the tough, slangy, or, as it was called, "debunking" style popular at the time. This work, produced in 1933, lampoons the two houses of the United States Congress by suggesting that personal and regional concerns carry more weight with legislators than the national interest. Yet Anderson does not make a scathing attack on the system of American government; indeed, as the play ends, he seems quite willing to leave matters much as they are. More characteristic in form though similar in point of view are his historical plays, a large body of work, most of which he wrote in blank verse in a lonely effort to restore poetry to the theater. Although he employed the past to illuminate the present, he nevertheless described it nostalgically, as though wishing to escape into it from present reality. Much as his protest against the inefficiency of politicians in *Both Your Houses* is stifled by comedy, the protests against governmental tyranny or industrial gigantism in *Night over Taos, Valley Forge, The Star-Wagon,* and the fantasy scenes of *High Tor,* to mention only a few plays, are stifled by romanticism. *Winterset,* a play on the aftermath of the Sacco-Vanzetti case, suffers from the same defect; the dialogue is too high-sounding for the events it describes. But at least it may be said that through all these plays Anderson gives evidence of his awareness of contemporary difficulties. At the end of the decade, in *Key Largo,* he made the obvious but well-meaning gesture of drawing a parallel between gangsters and Fascists.

S. N. Behrman is not only a more amusing writer than Anderson but also more complex. His personality is curious but by no means rare among men of letters: a combination of political liberalism and social snobbery. If his plays are to be taken as revelations of his own feelings, possessors of great wealth are the only persons who compel and sustain his interest. It is true that many persons without means make attractive appearances in his plays, but only if they are within the social orbit of their economic superiors. His comedies of manners, all good theater, glance back to the 1920's in their scenes of simple intrigue among persons to whom wealth has always come easily. A man of his time nevertheless, Behrman incorporated social themes in all his plays of the 1930's. In *Rain from Heaven* and *Wine of Choice,* respectively, he exposed adherents to the far right and left as the enemies of wit and promise. Bespeaking his own uncertainty about the American political outlook, he created in *End of Summer* a charming woman of wealth who, on the threshold of middle age, wishes to provide subvention for a politically progressive journal so as to make, in the words of the editor, "a perpetual dedication to Youth—to the hope of the world." To his credit, then, Behrman did not allow his success with comedy to beguile him into complacency. As the decade closed, he offered in *No Time for Comedy* a kind of public airing of his thoughts on his own talent. The protagonist of the play is, like Behrman himself, a writer of high comedy; as the international situation worsens, he—and again, one assumes, like Behrman himself—wonders whether comedy is a valid form of entertainment in such an age. After an abortive attempt at supposedly more serious drama, he decides to write a play about his own confusion. It is to be a comedy.

Robert E. Sherwood, on the other hand, made a successful shift from high comedy to, if not tragedy, drama of arrestingly serious import. From *Reunion in Vienna* in 1931, a highly praised comedy bringing into question the theories of psychoanalysis, he turned, four years later, to a pessimistic survey of the Depression scene in *The Petrified Forest.* The play is not a theatrical landmark, but it stands out as the best realized of the comparatively few Depression dramas expressing a negative view. It does not offer even the limited solace of a cautionary tale. It is a picture of America, set to particular purpose in the Western desert, in which no hope is to be derived from any political philosophy, in which spiritual values are dead. Sherwood's protagonist is a writer who, having found no comforting ideals in contemporary life, wanders through the desert with a copy of essays by Jung titled in English *Modern Man in Search of Soul;* at his own wish he is killed by a gangster, Sherwood's symbol of materialism at its most obsessive. *Idiot's Delight,* produced two years later, is set at the outbreak of the war which Sherwood recognized was certain to come soon. The playwright brings together in an Alpine hotel representatives of the major nations and political philosophies. Through their disputes his conviction emerges that the humanitarian instinct has been smothered by chauvinism and man's zeal for economic gain; at the play's end two sympathetic Americans wait for death under bombardment, singing "Onward, Christian Soldiers" at the piano. The profound pessimism of the two plays would seem nearly incurable, so strongly is it expressed. Yet Sherwood followed them in 1938 with an astonishingly affirmative historical play, *Abe Lincoln in Illinois.* As with Anderson's work, this is a nostalgic view of the past, with occasional pauses for laughter, but it has a theme for the time. Through Lincoln's refusal to compromise on the slavery issue regardless of the cost, Sherwood asserts that man at all times must summon the courage to fight for the banishment of evil. Under this theme lay the belief that *evil could be banished.* Like the great majority of American intellectuals, Sherwood had taken an interventionist position as Europe prepared for war.

To repeat, I have called attention to these three writers because they were at once social dramatists *and* skilled craftsmen, not because their plays are typical of the work of their generation. Other experienced dramatists of that generation, such playwrights as Elmer Rice and John Howard Lawson, were far more militant and much less successful; this is particularly true of Lawson, whose revolutionary zeal proved intolerable to audiences. Others, such as Philip Barry and Marc Connelly, were all but indifferent (as dramatists) to shifts in social thought and yet wrote popular plays. George S. Kaufman, who with various collaborators was perhaps the most financially successful playwright of the 1930's, touched only lightly on significant issues until the end of the decade when, with Moss Hart, he offered a patriotic, anti-Nazi play, *The American Way,* which was as much admired as any of his farces. Eugene O'Neill and Thornton Wilder, America's most distinguished playwrights, did not concern themselves at all with problems new to the 1930's. But the plays of Anderson, Behrman, and Sherwood, if not representative, are an impressive contribution to the American repertory. The work of sensitive, urbane men, they contrast sharply with the equally popular plays of the younger writers of the decade.

Dour and angry though it is, the social drama of writers new to the stage in the 1930's is almost unfailingly confident. Hopefulness is, to be sure, a quality possessed by youth in every age, for the young are eternally certain that they can remake the world in accordance with their own standards of justice. Young writers of the 1930's, observing economic distress on all sides, believed in their ability to create a milieu in which the spirit could flourish, unburdened by materialistic considerations. Striking out at the complacency of their elders, they expected to move through indignation to dignity. Often naïve in their self-confidence, they nevertheless produced a drama of extraordinary vitality.

In the first half of the decade, young rebels of the Marxist persuasion chose as models for their plays the short agitational dramas produced by European workers' troupes in the 1920's. Originally, such plays were designed to show the victory of the workers over their employers, who were always depicted as inhumanly aggressive. At the outset, the workers, unlike their employers, have no organization; in due course, however, they band together under a leader and forcefully demand better wages. The American writers expanded this simple structural scheme to accommodate a wide range of social theses. Tense, tough, and vivid, depicting forces of evil in heated argument with forces of good, their plays bear titles that even now evoke the issues, domestic and foreign, of their time—*Scottsboro Limited* by Langston Hughes, on race relations; *Dimitroff* by Elia Kazan and Art Smith, on the Reichstag fire; *Waiting for Lefty* by Clifford Odets, on labor unions; and, a longer play, *Panic,* by Archibald MacLeish, on bank failures. These are, of course, only four plays out of dozens, and are mentioned because of the prominence of their authors. Telegraphic dialogue gave way to naturalistic scenes in *Dimitroff* and *Lefty,* and simple patterned groupings of actors evolved into choreographed movement resembling dance in *Panic. Waiting for Lefty* became one of the most popular plays of the decade; its final emotional appeal for a strike of "stormbirds of the working-class" brought to their feet hundreds of theatergoers who were by no means radical in their political views.

Most such plays were produced for very short runs, however, and rarely on Broadway. After 1935 few were written. For such writers as Hughes and Odets they were apprentice work, though substantial enough in their own right. Recognizing that the anticipated class war was not, after all, inevitable, radical playwrights abandoned overt Marxist messages along with the dramatic form in which they had delivered them. They took as their favorite theme one which had proved serviceable to writers since the beginning of the economic downturn: the obligation of the individual to renounce self-interest for the good of his fellow man. Should the protagonist of a play on this theme forswear ambition at an early point in his career, peace of mind was his for the rest of his life; but should he obtain his goal of wealth or power, he was fated either to die before the final curtain or to fall victim to enduring unhappiness. With or without happy endings, the plays were optimistic, because they demonstrated their authors' beliefs that the audience could take example from the dramatic characters and follow a socially constructive course of action. In many works of the decade, this theme is embodied in a contest between youth and age. The settings, which adhere to the conventional walled-in realism dominant in the American theater since the 1890's, are such familiar environments as the home, the office, and the school.

Of the Depression playwrights, it was Clifford Odets who most firmly held the public imagination. Only twenty-eight when *Waiting for Lefty* was first produced, he wrote with such ardor and intensity as to seem still younger. Not an intellectual, he dramatized the economic crisis in terms of the actions and feelings of very ordinary persons; the relatively few complex characters in his plays lack credibility. Yet intellectuals—and especially young intellectuals—found it easy to identify with him. In *The Fervent Years* his friend and colleague, Harold Clurman, has described the effect of *Waiting for Lefty* at the final moment of its first performance:

> When the audience at the end of the play responded to the militant question from the stage: "Well, what's the answer?" with a spontaneous roar of "Strike! Strike!" it was something more than a tribute to the play's effectiveness, more than a testimony of the audience's hunger for constructive social action. It was the birth cry of the thirties. Our youth had found its voice. It was the call to join the good fight for a greater measure of life in a world free of economic fear, falsehood, and craven servitude to stupidity and greed. "Strike!" was *Lefty*'s lyrical message, not alone for a few extra pennies of wages or for shorter hours of work, strike for greater dignity, strike for a bolder humanity, strike for the full stature of man.

Never again would Odets be quite so outspoken, but he still had something to ask of the world, and youth was to become his spokesman.

Always a sentimentalist, Odets believed that the young had that special vision to see, all at a glance, the heart of a problem and its solution. Yet the solution, as his characters phrase it, is vague. Plan! organize! be active!—these are the recommendations of his young people; but the means of doing all this and the reason for doing it they only partly understand. Three of them are memorable characters—Ralph Berger in *Awake and Sing!*, Joe Bonaparte in *Golden Boy*, and Cleo Singer in *Rocket to the Moon*—but more memorable as curious, engaging human beings than as prophets of the better life.

Awake and Sing!, produced in 1935, describes the tensions arising within a lower-middle-class family, the Bergers of the grimly depressed Bronx, whose generations cannot agree on the ultimate values of life. Bessie Berger, the matriarch, is determined to keep the family intact and financially secure. Her methods are as ruthless as those of any industrial titan as such a figure might be conceived by a propagandist of the left. She arranges a marriage for her pregnant daughter to a man who is not the child's father, disrupts her son's love affair, and so bedevils her mildly reproachful father that the man commits suicide to escape her. She is money-mad, because only with money can the family be safe— safe from the threat of dispossession and the neighbors' gossip. Her acceptance of materialistic values has made a monster of a woman who in another culture might have been an affectionate wife and mother. When it is revealed that her father left three thousand dollars in insurance to her son Ralph, Bessie is forced to defend her ways, lest the boy in fury take the money and leave the family. In the accents of the urban community, she declares: "On the calendar it's a different place, but here without a dollar you don't look the world in the eye. Talk from now to next year—this is life in America." Odets makes no attempt to justify her ways— he wishes merely to explain them. It is up to Ralph, who is scarcely out of his boyhood, to speak for the opposition: "I'm not blaming you, Mom. Sink or swim—I see it. But it can't stay like this." With his enthusiasm for change at fever pitch, he declares that starting at once in the warehouse where he works he and other young people will alter the course of American life—in his words: "Maybe we'll fix it so life won't be printed on dollar bills." But how to do this? Odets evades the question. It was sufficient for him, and for his audience, to believe that the young *could* do it. Apart from his zeal, Ralph would seem to have no weapon whatever, unless it be labor's traditional means of redress, the strike.

Having given up the insurance money for the good of his family, Ralph can afford to feel happy. He has arrived at joy through self-denial. As much may be said for Leo Gordon, an older man, in Odets' *Paradise Lost*. But the life of Joe Bonaparte, the young protagonist of *Golden Boy,* is as predictably unhappy as Ralph's is joyous. At the beginning of manhood he commits the kind of act known contemptuously in the 1930's as "the sell-out." He must decide whether to continue to study the violin, his first love, in preparation for a career on the concert stage, or to become a prizefighter. His choice is boxing, since the fight ring offers the better chance of financial success. On the eve of his twenty-first birthday he explains his decision: "Every birthday I ever had I sat around. Now'sa time for standing. Poppa, I have to tell you—I don't like myself, past, present, and future. Do you know there are men who have wonderful things from life? Do you think they're better than me? Do you think I like this feeling of no possessions? . . . You don't know what it means to sit around and watch the months go ticking by! Do you think that's a life for a boy my age? Tomorrow's my birthday! I change my life!" Odets' tactics in the play are obviously extreme. His symbol for the battle for material possessions, professional boxing, is immensely brutal; his symbol for spiritual values, the art of the violin, is utterly delicate. It is most improbable, as critics of the play have observed, that one man might excel at both. Yet the audience of the thirties was no more inclined to question this straining after metaphor than it was to question the fiery but vain threats and promises of Ralph Berger in *Awake and Sing!,* nor could the audience react in cynicism to the sudden ending of Joe's career in *Golden Boy,* when, after killing an opponent in the ring, he drives off into the night and crashes fatally into a tree. If this was suicide, so be it—it was inevitable. Had Joe listened to his father, an old Italian immigrant untouched by the ways of his adopted country, all might have ended happily. Joe came to understand the problem of his time, but too late.

In his last work of the decade, *Rocket to the Moon,* Odets returned to the evangelical mood of *Awake and Sing!* The play provides another declamatory young person of the sort who, in the vision of the playwright, could turn the nation toward spiritual goals. For the first time, it is a girl who shows the way. Although at the core of her being Cleo Singer is as unselfish as Ralph, she has one great demand to make of life and will not be defeated in her determination to secure it. Hers is not a dangerous desire—it is love. This is the ultimate value and its importance rests in the fact that it is a shared experience. Turning her back on her two suitors, one who is middle-aged and married and the other who is his elderly, libidinous father-in-law, she announces her plan for the future: "Yes, if there's roads, I'll take them. I'll go up all those roads till I find what I want. I want a love that uses me, that needs me. Don't you think there's a world of joyful men and women? Must all men live afraid to laugh and sing? Can't we sing at work and love our work? It's getting late to play at life; I want to *live* it. Something has to feel real for me, more than both of you. You see? I don't ask for much. . . ." But what she wants represents, in her words, "a whole full world, with all the trimmings." It was the conviction of Odets that the young were deserving of a whole, full world, and he did his part in encouraging them to try for it.

A more realistic view of mankind's prospects is present in the plays of Lillian Hellman, who in critical and popular favor was second only to Odets among the social dramatists of the 1930's. Although only one year older than Odets, she seemed from the outset of her career to possess a steady, mature intellect. In her two great successes of the Depression years, *The Children's Hour* and *The Little Foxes,* she expressed the belief that those whose social attitudes she despised were too tough and too experienced to be swept aside by nothing more than the rhetoric of protest. She did not recommend open rebellion. If her plays agitate against evil, they do so by the indirect method of holding it up to view, not by the direct means of a militant appeal.

Although the production of her first play did not cause a stampede in the theater, it was not lacking in shock effect. *The Children's Hour,* produced in 1934, is a painful study of the tyranny of the aged and wealthy over the young and poor. To present this theme, Miss Hellman developed a plot involving allegations of homosexual love between two women. Undoubtedly the references to homosexuality, much rarer in drama then than now, brought curiosity-seekers to the theater, but Miss Hellman did not treat the subject sensationally; she might, indeed, have chosen any other type of immoral conduct and kept her theme intact. The two young women who are rumored to be in love with each other are attempting to run a small boarding school for girls; having very little money, they must calculate their expenditures carefully. A neurotic, conscienceless pupil starts the gossip concerning them, and, although it is based on very flimsy evidence, it is enough to ruin them. The child's grandmother, a woman of power in the district, believes and broadcasts the lie. The trouble with this woman is twofold: she is both old and rich, a member of a generation used to having its own way, of making its own truths. The ending of the play reveals the extent of her power. One victim of the lie admits that although nothing overtly erotic has occurred, she has long felt a romantic attachment to her friend. Her only recourse is suicide. The old woman is appropriately sorry for what she has done, but her remorse is quite obviously futile. She will suffer bitterly in her remaining years—thus the playwright takes her revenge.

In *The Little Foxes,* produced in 1939, Miss Hellman wrote with still greater severity; again she was reluctant to suggest a solution to the problems imposed on mankind by the misuse of money and position. In the very act of writing the play she revealed her wish for a change in popular values, but her plot offers no comforting thought that it will take place tomorrow. Set in the

South at the beginning of the century, the play offers in its central role a woman grotesquely ambitious for wealth. By the most ruthless means, including the refusal to bring medicine to her dying husband, she gains control of a family business. Thus she can become, in the language of the play, "big rich," and avenge the snubs delivered to her all her life by the more genteel families of the community. Her appalling greed costs her the love of her daughter, but the loss does not seem to dull her triumph. Despite its many scenes of cruelty, *The Little Foxes* is a play of stunning impact. Seldom has the evil of materialism received such detailed characterization as in Miss Hellman's monstrous protagonist.

It would be no more honest to claim that Clifford Odets and Lillian Hellman are typical of the generation of playwrights of the 1930's than to claim that Anderson, Behrman, and Sherwood are typical of the playwrights of the 1920's. I have focused on them because of the security of their position in American theatrical history as social dramatists. Their works project, beyond those of their contemporaries, the pungency, the ferocity, and the sense of righteous indignation that have come to seem the very feel of the 1930's. Without question, it is Miss Hellman who is the more impressive dramatist, by virtue of her avoidance of the easy answer; her plays have a life outside the context of the Depression years. Moreover, her art continues to develop in admirable though infrequent contributions to the stage. The work of Odets, on the other hand, has already become dated. Its topicality is a guide to us today in our effort to understand the Depression milieu, but discourages producers from reviving the plays. We must not complain, however; every age creates works which later reward us in the library, where we may stop, think, and reread, though they fail to return to life in the theater.

Despite the extensive changes in American life since World War II, the social dramatists of the 1930's continue to exert an influence. Our most respected postwar playwrights, Tennessee Williams and Arthur Miller, achieved their first successes with plays written under the shadow, so to speak, of the prewar years; Williams' *The Glass Menagerie* and Miller's *All My Sons* are plays of family tensions in which the authors champion the right of youth to rebel against the muddled world of their parents. William Inge, until recently a serious rival for attention, has shown somewhat less concern over economic insecurity, but has brought it into every play nevertheless. For these writers, all of whom came of age in the 1930's, materialism is a permanent target. Although they have begun to give greater weight to psychological motivation than to more narrowly social issues, they refuse to take prosperity for granted. Like the Depression writers, they ask the biblical question: "For what is a man profited, if he shall gain the whole world and lose his own soul?" The difference in approach is that their characters have gained the world before the rise of the curtain and on first entrance reveal that their souls are lost, whereas the characters of the 1930's gained or foreswore the world midway through the action and lost or saved their souls accordingly. Since 1959 still younger playwrights, of whom James Baldwin and the late Lorraine Hansberry are the most notable, have provided a number of plays on the plight of the American Negro which summon memories of the 1930's by the bluntness of their appeals. They are highly charged, aggressive plays, but, unlike most agitational drama of old, they serve an undeniably worthy end.

PART II

The Big Time

4 BROADWAY AFTER WORLD WAR II

Elliot Norton

In the period since World War II, the Broadway theater has discovered and developed two significant new dramatists, Tennessee Williams and Arthur Miller, and one young playwright of great promise, Edward Albee, and has produced a number of admirable musical plays and a great many musical comedies—some of them banal and dreary—a few slick, frivolous comedies, a handful of dramas of some distinction, and a considerable amount of trash.

In the same period, its playgoers and critics rediscovered and reevaluated Eugene O'Neill. In 1956, three years after his death, they reinstated him as the foremost American writer of plays principally on the basis of his long autobiographical drama *Long Day's Journey into Night*.

Williams was the first of the new writing stars to shine over Broadway. On March 31, 1945, *The Glass Menagerie* introduced him to those theatergoers of New York who make and break careers in our theater. With Laurette Taylor starred as Amanda Wingfield in a performance of great insight and tenderness, his first play was not only accepted but acclaimed. It became a popular hit, and is now established as one of the few classics of American theater, played by companies of professionals or amateurs all over the United States, sometimes well, sometimes badly, but always with success.

Arthur Miller, who had begun his career earlier with a play that failed, proved himself on Broadway in 1947 with a tough-minded melodrama called *All My Sons*. Two years later, his

Death of a Salesman all but overwhelmed the New York audience and it, too, took its place as an American classic despite the feverish objections of certain critics.

Edward Albee, who had got his first hearing off-Broadway with such one-act plays as *The Zoo Story,* was graduated to the commercial playhouses in 1962. His first full-length drama, *Who's Afraid of Virginia Woolf?,* stirred a great commotion, in which praise for its obvious power was mingled with anger over its brutality, and, in some quarters, indignation at the unusual candor of its language. In the midst of the controversy, the general public began to buy tickets in great quantities. *Virginia Woolf* became the first and, thus far, the only popular success of Edward Albee.

The story of Eugene O'Neill's new acceptance in the postwar period is rather unusual. He had been generally, though not universally, accepted in the 1920's as the foremost dramatist of the United States, and his reputation had been endorsed abroad. Three times in less than fifteen years he was awarded the Pulitzer Prize for the "best American play of the year." In 1936 he received the Nobel Prize for Literature, the first American playwright to be so honored.

Two years before the Nobel honor was conferred on him, O'Neill withdrew from New York to concentrate on what was to have been his greatest project, the writing of a cycle of plays about a fictional American family whom he would pick up in the eighteenth century and carry into the twentieth. Between 1934 and 1946, when he returned to New York, he wrote and discarded at least five of the proposed cycle plays, and completed just one, *A Touch of the Poet,* and found time to write two or three others outside the cycle, among them *The Iceman Cometh* and *Long Day's Journey into Night.*

Iceman and *Poet* were ready for production in 1946. *Long Day's Journey into Night* he consigned to a publisher, with instructions that it was not to be published (he made no mention of production) for twenty-five years after his death—this because it deals intimately with his own private family life; with himself, his brother Jamie, and his mother and his father, very thinly concealed under the name Tyrone.

The Theatre Guild presented *The Iceman Cometh* with James Barton starred as Hickey, the evangelical hero, in an atmosphere of unprecedented anticipation. Seventy-four critics, representing newspapers all over the United States and Europe, were in the first-night audience, to see and appraise the first new O'Neill play since *Days without End* in 1934. The critical verdict was sharply divided and the play was not a commercial success. Nine years later, in an off-Broadway production that starred Jason Robards, Jr., then almost unknown, as Hickey, it won acceptance as a major O'Neill work and this led to the production, with his widow's permission, of *Long Day's Journey into Night* on Broadway. There were no differences of opinion about this one. Critics and public were enthusiastic now, and a new vogue for O'Neill began.

Meanwhile, Williams had again proved his power to both press and public in such plays as *A Streetcar Named Desire* and *Cat on a Hot Tin Roof,* and Arthur Miller had won some, though not very much, enthusiasm for *The Crucible* and then, after [nine] years away from the stage, a mixed reception for *A View from the Bridge* which was produced in 1955.

In the meantime the Broadway theater of comedies and farces had flourished. Musical comedy, the most popular of all forms, was attracting larger and larger crowds and in certain conspicuous instances was giving way to something better, the musical play.

Musical comedy began to be called by that name just after the beginning of the twentieth century. It was—and still is—a simple romantic entertainment derived in part from operetta and in part from those elaborate nineteenth-century shows called "extravaganzas." It presented—and still presents—young men in ardent pursuit of young women, frustrated by misunderstanding but ultimately triumphant. It is innocent, often naïve, plagued by stereotypes but brightened, at its best, by tuneful songs, lively dances, and modest jokes, all sung, danced, and played by personable people and directed by showmen whose skill sometimes amounts to brilliance.

The musical play is like musical comedy, but its authors and composers have tried to do away with stereotypes, to substitute credible characters for "types," to integrate libretto, song, and dance, and to achieve genuine dramatic effects instead of merely soothing or titillating the audience. Although the term "musical play" was not formally used until *South Pacific* in 1949, the form had been developing alongside of musical comedy since Maxwell Anderson wrote *Knickerbocker Holiday,* with music by Kurt Weill, eleven years earlier. It gained new impetus when Weill collaborated in 1941 with Moss Hart to create in *Lady in the Dark* a popular entertainment whose characters were something better than typical heroes and heroines and whose music and dancing were integral to the libretto. Rodgers and Hammerstein took further action in behalf of the new form in *Oklahoma!,* two years later, blending song, dance, and story. In 1945, the year World War II ended, they offered to Broadway their *Carousel,* the first of the true musical plays and one of the most memorable.

Like most of the others which have followed, *Carousel* was not created but adapted; Oscar Hammerstein's libretto is an American version of Ferenc Molnár's *Liliom.* But the flavor is American, the characters have some validity as representatives of the human race, and the best of the songs are organic to the play. Since *Carousel,* there have been many old-style musical comedies adhering to the old formula which *Sally* and *Sunny* and so many others followed in the twenties and the thirties. And there will be many more in the future, for an increasingly large part of the Broadway audience insists on checking its mind and its deeper emotions in the lobby along with its coats and hats. But musical plays have also been written from time to time, and most of the best of them have found an audience in the commercial theaters of New York and elsewhere. The best include *Brigadoon,* one of the few with an original story, written by Alan Jay Lerner with music by Frederick Loewe; *South Pacific* and *The King and I,* both by

Rodgers and Hammerstein; Cole Porter's *Kiss Me, Kate*; *My Fair Lady*, by Lerner and Loewe; *West Side Story*, by Arthur Laurents, with lyrics by Stephen Sondheim and music by Leonard Bernstein, and the most recent, *Fiddler on the Roof*, which was adapted by Joseph Stein from some of the short stories of Sholom Aleichem.

West Side Story is an admirable example of the new form. It follows the older pattern of musical comedy in that its young hero and heroine fall in love at first sight and then struggle against misunderstanding. It departs in that they are not ultimately joined in matrimony: he is killed. Then, in a drastic variation from the formula, the remaining principals follow his coffin at the end. *West Side Story*, just as the conventional shows, has its share of love songs—like "Maria"—but its story is not just prettily romantic; it is socially significant. Its heroine is a Puerto Rican girl of New York's West Side, its hero a native American. Their romance parallels that of Shakespeare's Romeo and Juliet, but it adds a modern racial clash. It is not merely set to music but to dance as well—an appalling street fight between racial gangs, a "rumble" as it is called by the young hoodlums, was choreographed by Jerome Robbins to fit the pattern of the play and to make it not only stirring but significant.

Although there are still many song-and-dance shows on Broadway that show no influence of the musical play, most of those that have been popular in the years since *Carousel* have been affected to some extent. *Hello, Dolly!*, for example, which seems in many ways to be a throwback to the first decade of the twentieth century, which introduces its title song with no more excuse than a cue in the orchestra pit; which derives its dance routines from ancient and discarded conventions, owes something to the new movement. Its libretto is concerned, of course, with love; that is obligatory. But it is calculated love, not the boy-meets-girl kind. It actually jeers at the conventions of romance. In the end, when she has bamboozled him into an agreement of matrimony, its heroine embraces not the hero, but the cash register in his store.

Twenty-five years ago, that ending would have been unthinkable in the theater of musical comedy.

The Broadway audience has changed since 1945, but not for the better. Although postwar playgoers have patronized *West Side Story* and *Carousel* their tastes are often dubious. They show little interest in drama of serious purpose and almost none in plays which dare depart from conventional form.

Thornton Wilder's *The Matchmaker* won critical endorsement on Broadway, but it split the public into two camps, one of which resented its characters' habit of stepping out of character to address the audience. Not until it acquired songs and dances and a new title, *Hello, Dolly!*, were they ready to accept its departures from their norms.

Robert Bolt's *A Man for All Seasons* pleased New York audiences despite its Brechtian techniques, but none of Brecht's own plays have. Despite academic endorsement and textbook approval, the German dramatist has been rejected in the commercial theaters of New York from the time of *Galileo,* which Charles Laughton produced in 1947, to *Mother Courage* in 1963.

As a matter of fact, few European dramatists except the late Jean Giraudoux have found favor in the commercial theater of New York. The French dramatist, who was introduced to the popular American audience before the war in S. N. Behrman's *Amphitryon 38,* had a Broadway hit in *The Madwoman of Chaillot* in 1948 and in Maurice Valency's adaptation of *Ondine* in 1953, and two years later a modest success with *Tiger at the Gates.*

Jean Anouilh, on the other hand, has proved too tart for the taste of Broadway playgoers who accepted *The Waltz of the Toreadors* for a modest engagement, enjoyed *The Lark* as Lillian Hellman revised it, were only mildly interested in *Becket,* although it co-starred Laurence Olivier and Anthony Quinn, and rejected altogether such other works as *Mlle. Colombe* and, in 1964, *The Rehearsal.*

With Alfred Lunt and Lynn Fontanne starred in a version that departed considerably from the original, Friedrich Duerrenmatt's

The Visit had a considerable run, but his *Romulus* failed completely.

Like Brecht, Samuel Beckett has been rejected by Broadway. Two productions of *Waiting for Godot* failed in the downtown theaters, one in 1956, which starred the great revue comedian Bert Lahr, as Gogo; another the following year with an all-colored cast.

Although his work has been endorsed in the little playhouse off-Broadway, none of Jean Genet's plays has even been attempted in the commercial theaters.

Eugene Ionesco has had one significant Broadway production. With the great comedian Zero Mostel starred, his *Rhinoceros* ran for 240 performances in a major playhouse. But the other works of Ionesco have been presented off-Broadway, or not at all.

Camus, Sartre, and Max Frisch have failed to interest the Broadway public, though they have been studied with some avidity in the universities and endorsed in various little-theater productions in New York and elsewhere. Albert Camus' *Caligula,* in a production of some pretensions, ran for thirty-eight performances. With Charles Boyer starred, under the English title *Red Gloves,* Jean-Paul Sartre's *Les Mains Sales* was rejected. Max Frisch's *Andorra* lasted for only one week.

In the twenties and thirties Broadway audiences, which were excited about O'Neill, Anderson, Robert E. Sherwood, and Clifford Odets, would very likely have supported these modernists of the postwar European theater. But their counterparts of the sixties have either been priced out of the big playhouses, or have found a new and greater stimulation in the art movies. Their places have been taken by the newly rich, or newly wealthy, a large group; by members of "theater parties," who in the name of charity pay high prices to go to the theater and subsequently write off the ticket prices on their income taxes; by those who come to New York for business and are either living on unlimited expense accounts or are given tickets to the Broadway hits by companies who expect to sell them something; and by rank-and-file tourists, most of whom see no theater in their own cities but

47

are willing to pay a big price to attend the shows in New York so they can tell the neighbors back home.

Those who go with the theater parties, which contribute more than a million dollars a year at the Broadway ticket windows, are guided by a group of eight or ten agents, to whom scripts are now submitted in advance by nervous play producers. These party-goers have become an important factor in the economy of Broadway. They are interested, like all the other special groups, in nothing but the lightest, most frivolous kind of entertainment. Few playgoers, as a matter of fact, are interested in anything else in the Broadway theater of the moment. And few producers are willing or able to take the huge financial risks involved in putting on plays that are less than conventionally entertaining.

Before the war it was possible to produce a play for eight or ten thousand dollars. Today, the producer must raise at least ten times that amount. During the prewar period, some producers dedicated themselves to plays of unusual merit, plays that reflected something of the rapidly changing life of our times. Most of these men have stopped production, or have curtailed their output. The Theatre Guild, once the boldest of them all, is now no more than a booking agency for its subscribers, forced by the colossal cost of production to avoid all risks.

That Broadway still exists in the face of continually rising costs, that audiences can still be found for the hits despite the mounting price of tickets and the competition of art movies and television, is something of a wonder. That it produces an occasional musical play of some distinction is heartening. That it has nurtured the best works of a handful of playwrights such as Williams, Miller, and O'Neill is encouraging. And that it will accept from time to time an occasional newcomer such as Edward Albee, or Murray Schisgal, the author of the unusual comedy called *Luv*, is encouraging, too.

The best of Broadway's new plays are the best produced in the United States: good or bad, we have no other true creative center in the drama. The best are often none too good. But we do have a

48

few to admire and even to cherish, and for the future we can hope. One of these days, perhaps, the tide will turn and a new wave of great young playwrights will appear, to find waiting for them on Broadway an alert, discriminating, and responsible young audience. It has happened before; it can happen again.

5 COMEDY AND THE COMIC SPIRIT IN AMERICA

Eric Bentley

It can be acknowledged from the outset that the play does not flourish in America as the novel and poem do. With the possible exception of Eugene O'Neill, the leading American dramatists do not rank with Melville, Twain, James, Faulkner, Hemingway, Emily Dickinson, Robert Frost, T. S. Eliot, Wallace Stevens, Robert Lowell.

And so it is that a writer who was spoken of at one time as America's Bernard Shaw—S. N. Behrman—is already almost forgotten. He has in fact none of the qualifications of Shaw: is not a writer of firstclass prose, is not a man of many or of interesting ideas, let alone a maker of durable plays. One might as easily speak of Noel Coward as the English Bernard Shaw, though passages in *Private Lives* are more scintillating than anything Behrman has written. The character of the American theater has been such—the American theater has been commercial to such an extent—that any writer with a modicum of Shaw's subtlety and seriousness would have turned to the novel to express himself. There is delightful comedy in many of the stories of Henry James, but when *Washington Square* was made into a play by other hands it became something less than either comedy or tragedy.

To speak only of the Bernard Shaws and Henry Jameses is to set our sights high. How many such writers are there anywhere at anytime? If America has produced little that is noteworthy in the way of drawingroom comedy, it has produced very many comic plays of other kinds that have delighted audiences not only in America but all around the world. Half a century ago comedy meant French comedy. Even when the author was not Labiche, or Feydeau, or one of their many French imitators, it was a non-French writer of their school. Are we today approaching a point where something of the sort could be said of American comedy? I don't think any single figure stands out like an American Labiche, but rather that a whole genre has imposed itself, so that almost any comic play that succeeds in New York goes on to succeed in the rest of the world. A play at present on the boards, *Luv* by Murray Schisgal, would be an example. There is something about the American comedies that tends to make the European ones seem a little staid and old-fashioned. The public flocks to American comedies to hear, as it were, a "new small talk," to dance to a new and more "exciting" rhythm.

One is reminded of the difference between operetta and American musical comedy. Masterpieces of operetta remain masterpieces whatever happens, but the operetta theater, in general, comes to seem faded and boring to a public that has seen *Oklahoma!* properly performed, though *Oklahoma!* is not a masterpiece. It's a case of the victory of the genre, and of a change in fashion. Not a season's change in fashion, either, but one of those radical changes, as from crinolines to short skirts, that set one era off from another.

Some of the better American comedies *are* musical comedies. I say this without having that prejudice in favor of the musical comedy which makes some of our New York newspaper critics rejoice at half a dozen examples of the genre every season. If you only see the shows that in some form or another reach England and continental Europe, then you are not seeing a representative but a superior selection. One season as a critic in New York would teach you that most musical comedies, though they may cost half a million dollars apiece, are very dull rubbish indeed. You emerge from them cursing the genre, not hailing it as the greatest American invention since federal democracy. So much effort, you cry, and so little result! Never did mankind owe so little to so many! But the best are good, and in a way that concerns the student of the comic spirit in America. Take *Guys and Dolls* or *Kiss Me Kate*. What's good about it? I don't think the merit of such a show can be localized in the script. Read the script, and you won't think of Oscar Wilde. I don't think the merit of such a show can be localized in the score: listen to the music, and you won't think of mentioning it in the same breath as Offenbach or *The Threepenny Opera*. But when all the parts are put together, the finished show has *pep, zing, zip,* and maybe even *oomph.* You can usually tell in the first few minutes if a musical comedy has this particular kind of aliveness. If it hasn't, it is alive in no fashion, and the half million dollars have been thrown away.

While on the subject of *Guys and Dolls,* let me tell a story. A few years ago I edited an anthology entitled *From the American Drama.* It put many people's backs up because all the serious playwrights from O'Neill to Arthur Miller were omitted. I was toying with the notion that serious American playwrights were generally second-rate Europeans, whereas the American contribution lay in the so-called lighter plays. And in musical comedies. This explains the inclusion in the book of *Guys and Dolls,* a musical comedy, which, I said, embodied "the American quality" very well. Now one of my most serious reviewers—too serious, maybe, to be the right man to review this book—observed that in representing *Guys and Dolls* to be especially American I was confusing America with New York City. Now it is true that I am not a native American, and I might be presumed to cherish a few European fallacies about the U.S., but I had not implied, or thought, either, that New York could be equated with America as a whole, as this critic supposed. However, New York is America in that it is certainly not Europe and does not resemble any European city any more than it resembles New Orleans or Minneapolis. And something of the character of New York is caught in the lingo of *Guys and Dolls.* The habitat of the lingo is in many spots unmistakable. Even that, though, is not what I had meant by "the American quality." This work has little or no value as a document. As a naturalistic study of milieu it is non-existent. For that matter, Damon Runyon, who wrote the story it is based on, and perfected this type of humor, was not a New Yorker at all, but a Southerner. In speaking of the American quality of this work, I am speaking of what sets it off from anything English or European—or Chinese. No non-American would fail to know just what I mean—or fail to agree that *Guys and Dolls* is inalienably American. So clearly so, as I said, that it is hard to get a plausible performance out of a non-American cast. It is a matter—one might put it—of how bottoms wiggle, or fail to wiggle. National character is in the behind. At any rate, it can most readily be spotted there. Ask an actor to walk across the stage: when he has done so, you know if he could appear in *Guys and Dolls*.

(In this respect Negro shows are only extreme instances of American shows. I have never seen anything more ludicrous than a European production of *Porgy and Bess,* done by white singers in black face. You knew their behinds weren't black. Perhaps Sir Laurence Olivier, in *Othello,* is the only European actor who ever seemed black all over, and he consumed so much energy in achieving this effect that some aspects of the role had to be sacrificed.)

As for *Guys and Dolls,* it draws upon the rhythm of American life—or, to be more precise, upon certain rhythms *in* American life—in order to create living theater. This is not at all the same as *describing* America. *Guys and Dolls* is in fact at several removes from the actual appearances of American life. But it is by no means unrelated to the reality. Certain features of the reality have been seized and brilliantly exploited. True, it is superficial, this *Guys and Dolls*. If indeed it were ever *not* superficial, it would tumble into bathos, as many musical comedies tumble into bathos when their creators sound off on race relations, education, or God. To forget God, and work with surfaces, can be a duty at times. Or as I think Humphrey Bogart once put it, leave messages to Western Union.

In what sense is musical comedy comedy? George Jean Nathan used to say the term was a misnomer, in that the typical musical comedy is not comic at all, but, on the contrary, highly lachrymose. What statistics would show I have no idea. Certainly the Rodgers and Hammerstein musical comedies could be cited in support of Nathan's view. But, of good musical comedies—good in Nathan's opinion or mine—a great many *are* in the comic tradition, especially if one grants that much non-musical comedy has been in some degree sentimental. Oscar Hammerstein seems to me to represent, not so much a permanent genre, as a phase in American history, the same phase as Norman Vincent Peale and President Eisenhower, a phase of humorless highmindedness, a phase of philistine goodwill and conformism. His predecessor as a collaborator with Rodgers, Lorenz Hart, had been another kettle of fish. Hart wrote comic lyrics, hard-hitting, free-wheeling comments on the more outrageous features of American life. That's *another* phase of American history, of course, and not necessarily more characteristic of musical comedy. But the name of Lorenz Hart can be used as the cue for a discussion of the social commentary in American comedy, musical or otherwise.

Comedy written within the framework of commercial America, Broadway or Hollywood, tends to pull its punches. Devastating accusations are made along the way, but in the end are withdrawn. The traditional happy ending of comedy, when assimilated by this pattern, tends to signify a kind of capitulation. Here is a satirist who started out in act one as a radical critic of society and then got scared in act three; the happy ending is a convention that enables him to creep, so to speak, to the cross. A thousand examples of this pattern could be given, and only a slightly less large number of dramatic critics failing to see the pattern. What such critics record is that Dramatist A, while seemingly a bit subversive and unsavory in the first act, turns out, along about 11 P.M., to have his heart in the right place.

Confronted with this phenomenon, the stern European critic can think of nothing but to rebuke the American dramatist for not keeping it up to the end. He assumes that a revision of the last twenty minutes of each play would set everything to rights. But a whole culture is involved in which commercial writers are selling the standard product. They are perfectly adjusted to things as they are and could no more afford to revise the last twenty minutes than they could afford to know that the last twenty minutes needed revising. The purely commercial artist in American society has a position like that of the purely official artist, the Party artist, in a totalitarian society. He is an example of *Gleichschaltung* or, if you prefer a Shakespearean image, of the dyer's hand taking on the color of the dye.

Better artists are *im*purely commercial or not commercial at all. Let me, in relation to comedy, and in relation to comedy that is satirical and makes a comment on society, mention responses of some better artists.

One kind of writer meets commercialism halfway. He expresses a willingness to work within the system, and this willingness is expressed in an acceptance of certain conventions. If there is satire against this or that, it may be presented as just the point of view of a single character; if it is more than that, it can be retracted in the happy ending. So far this better writer is indistinguishable from the inferior or totally adjusted writer. The difference emerges in the malaise everywhere perceptible in the better writer's work. Sometimes this is so great that a sentimental ending is insufficient as a counterweight. Think of such plays as *You Can't Take It with You*. It was the Marxist criticism of them that the unrest they embody and communicate is dissipated by a phony reconciliation at the end. The question is whether this criticism is merely doctrinaire. It looks right. It seems to fit. But when you go back to those plays—I don't want my argument to depend on my being right about *You Can't Take It with You,* in particular—you often find that the sentimental ending falls into place as an ironic insincere bow to conservatism, while the spirit of rebellion in the body of the play rings true.

That is one pattern. There is another, that the European more readily understands, because it is "consequent" and of a piece. Marc Blitzstein's *Cradle Will Rock* is an American musical comedy and at the same time a consistently Marxist study of society. No reconciliation at the end of this one—on the contrary! Now Blitzstein's piece is certainly one of the better American musicals.

If it is no masterpiece, that is because all too many compromises are made, not—in this case—on the political, but on the artistic front. The writing, especially, is limited by being wholly in a vulgar commercial mode. Perhaps the intention was to exploit clichés and transcend them, but to my mind the transcendence is very incomplete. And this has to do with the fact that Blitzstein's attitude, though it can be called extreme by those who think in political terms, was conventional and conformist in cultural, and so ultimately in human, terms. He did not rebel except politically, i.e., on the surface. On the contrary, he accepted most of what a real rebel would be rebelling against: the way of life, the way of feeling and thinking and behaving, of the established regime.

Marc Blitzstein was a Communist but it is not Communism I am objecting to: I can give an example of deeper rebellion in one who also has been inclined to Communist opinions, namely, Charlie Chaplin. And I make no apology for bringing Chaplin into the discussion, even though some people will have it that he is neither a dramatist nor an American. His work was done in America, and a large part of it was the creating of (cinematic) dramas. Are not the Chaplin films the supreme American comedies?

Chaplin represents, among many other things, rather thoroughgoing rebellion. Of the sentimental pseudo-solution of things he definitely makes a joke. If Americans have not understood his hankering after Communism, they have understood even less—in my opinion—what precedes it and explains it: that this successful man rejects the world which embraces him. Granted that he wanted the homage; one must concede also that he does not return it.

What I am alleging of Charlie Chaplin is more obviously true of W. C. Fields. And he too should be brought into the discussion, not so much because he often wrote his own scenarios, as because the discussion can justifiably pass from comedy to comedianship and even from comedianship to the comic spirit in America.

It has often been said of Fields that he is misanthropic, but, more specifically, he is a critic of what passes for the American way of life. Not even a critic. He is just against it. He thumbs his nose at it. He gives it a Bronx cheer. He takes up each idol of popular Americanism and breaks it—the baby and the child, the wife and the mother—everything that makes a house a home. And the American retreat and refuge from these—the whisky bottle—which in "square" American works has so often been shown as pathetic is here held up in bravado as a solution. Thus in the 1930's the most radical writer of American comedy—or, at any rate, the writer of the most radical American comedy—was not Marc Blitzstein but W. C. Fields.

Similarly, if one would name a "first lady" of American comedy, one should not pick a real lady like Katharine Cornell, nor yet a beautiful actress of drawingroom drama like Ina Claire, but rather Miss Mae West. Miss West has not been seen on stage all that often, but on the strength of her film appearances alone she was for a while the first lady of American comedy, just as, a little earlier, was Marie Dressler. Margaret Dumont, the dowager of the Marx Brothers films, is a lady of that same comic world, the principal comic world, probably, that America has created outside the novel.

When I praise Chaplin or Fields I am not praising their personal and special achievements alone. In that generation, there existed, if chiefly in the movies, an American comedy. The Marx Brothers afford another excellent example. Though not radical in the usual political sense, they are far more radical critics of society than the recognized radicals. The "American way of life" is rejected point by point. It is the bad joke from which they make their good jokes.

Today, *Doctor Strangelove* gives a Marx Brothers' view of the atomic age. At least what is good about it does. *Strangelove* has a weakness. It has something of the self-congratulatory cleverness of Private Eye and the current English school of the Devastating. The upshot of the sick jokes of this school is that they cancel themselves out. There is such a thing as becoming so radical that you find yourself a conservative again: you have rejected so much in theory that you accept everything in practice. Such is cynicism. *Strangelove* has the makings of a radical film but dwindles into a conformist one. It communicates the suspicion that its makers might in actuality decide that, since our generals are *not* crazy, they are entitled to drop the bomb. One might call this the spirit of appeasability. Whereas, W. C. Fields, though he is unpolitical, is unappeasable, implacable—"incorrigible," if you will.

I am speaking of the makers of the *Strangelove* film in the abstract, as if they were a harmonious team, and as if accident played no role. The novel *Candy* is better comedy, and consistently embodies the non-political radicalism I am talking about. It is the best American comedy of recent years in any genre, and it makes the most pertinent of comments on the current state of the American soul.

A final point. The comic element is often the best part of plays that, as a whole, are not considered comedies. This is particularly true of American plays, and, most particularly, of those of the two most prominent American playwrights of the present moment, Tennessee Williams and Edward Albee. Williams has often been admired for other, supposedly profounder elements, and when he has been condemned it has been on the grounds that the profundity was spurious. Those who do the condemning should, however, hasten to add that Williams has a fine comic sense and knows how to use it. The Father in *Cat on a Hot Tin Roof* is a comic figure in far more than the fact that he uses scandalous language. Comedy is here used for its classic purpose: to place people in their society, to define them as what Karl Marx said they are, the sum of their social relationships.

Is it not largely wit and humor that prevent both *Streetcar* and *The Glass Menagerie* from being unbearably sentimental? The confrontation of Blanche Dubois and Stanley Kowalsky is a brilliant comic *idea*, worked out, to be sure, to a pathetic conclusion. Even so, the pathetic conclusion is, artistically speaking, the least valuable part of the story. Of the Mother in *The Glass Menagerie,* the same may be said as of the Father in *Cat:* she constitutes a splendid social portrait. The same forthright method is used too—monologue, virtually—a torrent of characteristic words which define the character socially—by jokes. Conversely, the bad plays of Williams have good passages, *and these passages are all very funny.*

Of *Who's Afraid of Virginia Woolf?* and *Tiny Alice,* this much is relevant here. To both evenings in the theater, there is a good deal of fun, and there is an attempt to be deep about modern life. The attempt to be deep, in both cases, fails, *but the fun in both cases, is fun.* And of course there must be more to fun that works on such a grand scale than tricks of phrase, or adroitness with quips and gags. And there is. If Albee can't define what he feels to be the tragedy of modern people, while groping for such a definition he does write an effective comedy of modern life. It has been said that the dialogue of the man and wife in *Who's Afraid of Virginia Woolf?* is really the dialogue of two catty homosexuals. Those who say this have assumed that it disposes of both Mr. Albee and his play. But no: what amuses and interests us is that a married couple talk with the sick-slick cleverness of "fairies." This is finally a comment, not on Albee, and not on "fairies," but on married couples—there lies the social substance, and there lies the fun. Albee is holding up the mirror to nature, and showing something that was always funny: inversion of natural function. His comment is valid, I think, as a kind of social realism, and it achieves a kind of symbolism too, if not always the kind the playwright seems to be after. The confusion in sexuality symbolizes the American and modern confusion of identities.

In any event, the first act of *Virginia Woolf* is the funniest bit of playwriting in many years, and that must be my excuse for including it in a discussion of American comedy. The man in the street's definition of comedies is "plays that are funny." I was taught in school that this was a very poor definition. But I have remembered it. I have not remembered what they taught me was a good definition.

6 THORNTON WILDER

Malcolm Goldstein

If his occasional essays and the ephemera printed in obscure journals are set to one side, Thornton Wilder's published works are far fewer than might be expected from a man who has spent over forty years as a professional writer. They number only eleven compact volumes, six of fiction and five of drama, and two one-act plays published only in magazines. Yet on this small body of writing his reputation rests secure. It is no doubt true that three of America's Nobel Prize winners, O'Neill, Hemingway, and Faulkner, cast longer shadows; critics prefer them for their naturalism, and they would seem to have exerted a greater influence than Wilder on young writers. Yet Wilder's novels continue to draw readers, and his plays, each an affirmative expression of the values of the human experience, are now standard works in the American repertory. Those closest to him believe that every night of the year somewhere in the United States a performance of his masterpiece, *Our Town,* takes place.

Though nothing like the drama of his mature years, Wilder's first published pieces were plays. As an undergraduate at Oberlin College and Yale University in the second decade of the century, he set himself the curious task of writing sketches for three actors of only three minutes' playing time each. Within this constrictive form he demonstrated, in the somewhat obvious manner of the clever schoolboy, that he enjoyed comparative studies in litera-

This chapter is based on, and in part is a condensation of, the author's *The Art of Thornton Wilder,* © 1965 by the University of Nebraska Press.

ture and had accepted the principles of philosophic humanism. The diction is allusive, the action is moralistic, and the settings are fantastic or historical. In 1928 fourteen of the pieces, along with three new ones, were gathered into the volume titled *The Angel That Troubled the Waters and Other Plays*. On the printed page they have that quality which an earlier age would have described, without irony, as "edifying," but they are not plays for the stage. The dialogue, like the dialogue of most fledgling playwrights, is overblown, and the scenic requirements are too luxurious for any but the most extravagant of theaters. A longer play written at Yale, *The Trumpet Shall Sound*, also suffers from faulty language; the theme of God's infinite capacity for forgiveness is all but buried under resounding but empty phrases. This work was produced for a limited run in 1926 by the American Laboratory Theatre, an early off-Broadway company, but without success. In view of the meager spirit of these first trials of talent, the strength of the plays to come was all the more remarkable. Wilder continued, to be sure, in the tradition of genteel letters with his first three novels, *The Cabala* in 1926, *The Bridge of San Luis Rey* in 1927, and *The Woman of Andros* in 1930, but after the publication of the last he sought and found a style of his own.

That style is first, and powerfully, evident in the volume published in 1931 titled *The Long Christmas Dinner and Other Plays in One Act*. Of the six collected pieces, not all, however, show the new skill. *Queens of France, Love and How to Cure It,* and *Such Things Only Happen in Books* are in the old manner; that is, they are romantic plays requiring heavy scenery. The difference between this group and the remaining three plays in the book is more than striking. *The Long Christmas Dinner, Pullman Car Hiawatha,* and *The Happy Journey to Trenton and Camden* are the manifestations of an altogether fresh insight into dramatic method. Gone is the admiration for the unfamiliar setting and the highly polished phrase. Scenery, except for the barest essentials, is banished, and the language is quite ordinary American speech. Freed from his habits of excess, Wilder also demonstrates

61

a new freedom from convention in the manipulation of time and space. Each of the three plays has its own way of treating the problems imposed on narrative technique by the theater. In *The Long Christmas Dinner*, the life of three generations of a Midwestern family moves across the stage in half an hour as husbands, wives, daughters, daughters-in-laws, sons, and grandsons reveal through table talk the passing of the years. In *Pullman Car Hiawatha*, Wilder describes a trip through time and space in the nocturnal movement of a train from New York to Chicago; the cross-country ride requires only half an hour on stage, but it is a many-leveled experience including not only the sense of motion, but a report on the landmarks and social history of the territory over which the train passes. *The Happy Journey* is a daylight trip made by one family in an automobile. As the travelers ride through the state of New Jersey, they slow down or hasten the passage of time merely by dwelling longer on some roadside phenomena than on others. Having discovered the possibilities of anti-naturalism, Wilder made the most of them.

Striving for universality, the playwright not only abandoned the localized setting, but created characters with whom the American audience could easily identify. Unlike most anti-naturalistic dramatists, who use the actor to reveal a type by portraying, not the total man, but his ruling passion, Wilder embodies in the characters of the one-acts, the popular concepts—"images," in the current jargon—of persons with certain definite functions to perform in life. He presents the upper-middle-class family with its members revealed in relation to one another in highly familiar ways, such as the reminiscing widow and her respectful daughter-in-law, and the spoiled son and his irate father; the lower-middle-class family, with the religious mother and her blaspheming son; the sleeping-car porter, forever good-natured; the construction engineer, forever unintellectual; and so on, through a wide range of humanity. Clichés they may be, but because clichés issue from closely observed activity, they function well in each play as expressions of truths about human nature. All economic classes receive careful attention, and all face the same problem—the difficulty of finding a quiet moment for calm speculation on the meaning of experience.

The very familiarity of the characters and situations elicits a strong emotional response. The audience is at one with the grieving daughter Genevieve of *The Long Christmas Dinner* as she mourns her mother: "I never told her how wonderful she was. We all treated her as though she were just a friend in the house. I thought she'd be here forever." Similarly it shares in the sense of a wasted life voiced by a dying woman in *Pullman Car Hiawatha:* "Oh, I'm ashamed! I'm just a stupid and you know it. I'm just another American." Most moving of all is a line near the close of *The Happy Journey.* When the family of travelers, father, mother, son, and daughter, arrive at the home of an older daughter who has barely escaped death during the delivery of a still-born child, they pause and act out a brief scene. On seeing her father, the young convalescent woman embraces him and asks the remarkable question, "Are you glad I'm still alive, pa?" Into this line, composed of some of the homeliest words in the language, Wilder packs three of man's basic feelings: the desire for love, the fear of rejection, and the fear of death.

Wilder employed the principle of character-simplification without distortion in his next work, the novel *Heaven's My Destination,* published early in 1935. Although this now seems the best of Wilder's fiction, and one of the strongest American novels of the 1930's, originally it was a bleak failure with the public and critics. Wilder refused to admit to discouragement, but nevertheless announced—prematurely, as it turned out—that he would write no more fiction. In drama, he believed, it was possible to write without offering oneself as an editorial presence directing the audience to an examination of particular facets of the characters' minds. He now preferred to present his themes through words and actions alone and take the chance that the audience would be willing to listen, watch, and interpret on its own. The result of these deliberations was *Our Town,* produced in 1938, in which a bare stage and simple speech again proved their effectiveness.

It remains astonishing, after more than a quarter of a century, that a play so lacking in sensationalism as *Our Town* should prove so durable. Nothing heroic, shocking, exotic, or, for that matter, unfamiliar occurs in it. Yet such is the power of the play to reach the emotions that it shames sophisticated raillery. *Our Town* tells the story of two neighboring families named Gibbs and Webb who live in the small town of Grover's Corners, New Hampshire, at the beginning of the present century. Their lives are in no way special. Nothing has happened to them that might set them off either as heroes or as victims, and their town is just another spot in the cosmos. Yet for the very reason that it is an ordinary place, the town comes to represent all societies, and whatever happens to its inhabitants is an expression, in general terms, of the chief events in the lives of all people.

The scenes devised by Wilder are moments of eternity singled out for our attention and played against the panorama of infinity. The first act is called "The Daily Life" and offers such details as the early-morning milk delivery, the family breakfast, and the children's departure for school. Moving through the day from dawn until bedtime, at every turn the action distills poignancy from the commonplace, including even so unremarkable an occurrence as the children's struggle with homework. These New Englanders, engaged as they are in ordinary, mundane duties, are authentic representatives of the entire race. Similarly, the titles of the second and third acts, "Love and Marriage" and "Death," the latter only hinted at, not spoken, describe the fundamental material of existence.

Of the twenty-two characters who pass across the stage, most are present only to populate an arena whose principal actors are George Gibbs and Emily Webb, the older children of the two families. All are under the care of a benign character known as the Stage Manager, who informs us of the background and predicts the events to come. Through the conduct of the lives of George and Emily, which, as we see them on Wilder's bare stage, they lead in infinite space at a point in the vast continuum of time, emerges in little the general pattern of the human adventure. At the moments when they act out their personal joy and sadness, they forthrightly illustrate those emotions as they come to us all. They are allegorical figures, but, because what they represent is not a special quality or force but the complete sum of the human passions, and because also they speak in an ordinary manner without the usual self-consciousness of allegorical figures, they are completely absorbing as characters in their own right. In attending, so to speak, to the development of George and Emily, Wilder is concerned primarily with their virtues, but he does not omit the vices in the design of their personalities. Thus, for example, they delight in ice-cream sodas, delay over their school assignments, and plan ahead for a profitable farm. These interests are nothing less than the deadly sins of gluttony, sloth, and avarice, yet so softened as to round out the design without rendering the boy and girl unattractive. The point is that if we are to see ourselves in George and Emily, we must not be so dismayed that we avert our eyes. The two grow up in houses on adjacent properties, play together as children, fall in love with each other in adolescence, and marry as soon as they graduate from high school. Emily dies in childbirth after nine years of marriage, and as the play ends George grieves hopelessly beside her grave. That is all, but so basic to the life of every civilization is this simple story and the emotion it evokes that its theatrical impact is universally stunning.

Although no scene of the play is lacking in strength, one moment near the close is especially effective in the presentation of the theme. Emily, seated among the dead, wishes overwhelmingly to return to earth for a last glance. She is permitted to do so, but must choose a particular day of the past and must act as both spectator and participant. She returns, then, for a re-enactment of her twelfth birthday, but finds the experience unbearable. She recognizes that she has lived her life in vain, since at no point in it did she see that although it was made up of only familiar, day-to-day activities, it was full of marvels nevertheless—the marvels of ticking clocks, sunflowers, food and coffee, newly ironed dresses, and hot baths, as well as the love bestowed on her by her family.

With this scene we come to a point to which Wilder always directs us: the belief that the cause of man's unhappiness is not his failure to achieve or sustain greatness, but his failure to delight in the beauty of ordinary existence. The people of Grover's Corners are the sort whose effect upon the world is slight, since they never move away from their particular piece of the universe. But for that reason they are the personages whose lives most clearly reflect the marvelousness of the unheroic. The play is a tragedy insofar as it shows us a young woman who, for all her goodness, dies before her time, and an equally good young man who must grieve for her forever. But like all great tragedy it possesses an undercurrent of optimism, for the most intelligent members of the audience can gain insight into their own lives from Emily's harrowing return to earth, and act upon what they learn.

Late in 1938, less than a year after the first performance of *Our Town,* Wilder offered a light comedy, *The Merchant of Yonkers,* on the same theme. The play is an adaptation of a nineteenth-century Viennese folk comedy, Johann Nestroy's *Einen Jux will er sich machen,* which in turn is based on the Englishman John Oxenford's *A Day Well Spent.* Thus from Britain to Austria to America came the plot—in its final form a simple pattern of an indomitable woman of the 1880's who arranges life for the good of all, and of two young clerks who abandon their jobs in the provincial town of Yonkers for a glimpse of high life in New York City. Because of difficulties in the casting and direction, the play was a failure on its first appearance. In 1954 Wilder retitled it *The Matchmaker,* made a few small revisions of the text, and released it for production at the Edinburgh Festival, where it was well received. Subsequently it enjoyed lengthy runs in London and New York.

In *The Matchmaker,* to use the new title, Wilder's theme of the joy of life takes the form of a plea to common men to search for adventure. He does not, however, wish to prompt us to heroic, history-making action, but, as in *Our Town,* to urge us to be conscious of our pleasures as we experience them. The character who most effectively represents the affirmative spirit which Wilder believes we must all develop is Mrs. Dolly Levi, a widow who pretends to arrange a marriage between the prosperous merchant Horace Vandergelder and a mysterious friend, only to lay her own trap for him. For her, as for Vandergelder, money is all-important; she, however, seeks it for comfort, not, like the merchant, for a bogus kind of power. She is free, a person not held in check by ignoble ambition. In the metropolis the entire cast of characters, headed by Dolly and Vandergelder's clerks, have adventures which take place amid banging doors, crashing screens, expensive dinners, and disguises. Ultimately, of course, all works out for the best: Dolly wins Vandergelder, and the clerks win pretty girls and their employer's forgiveness for deserting his store in his absence.

For this comedy Wilder sought an entirely new presentational method. The play is a parody of the stock-company pieces with their pat endings that he saw as a boy in California. As such, it makes fun of the conventional box sets employed in the originals to house domestic situations—sets which suggest attitudes of smugness on the part of playwrights and audiences inasmuch as they prevent the great world outside from intruding on the characters' comfortable existence. Keeping the world at a distance from the slight characters of *The Matchmaker* as determinedly as he had drawn it in as a backdrop for the sturdy characters of *Our Town,* he called for four different interior sets to confine the action to specific locales. They hold us to the present moment on the stage, allowing no hint that a cruel, passionate humanity lives just the other side of the walls. For both professional productions of the play, the designers, presumably with the author's blessing, carried out the parody by painting flat, bright, conspicuously "charming" scenes which referred to but did not precisely mirror the style of the late nineteenth century. Still another mockery of convention is the device of permitting each major character to come forward and reveal his views on life directly to the audience

67

as though in conversation with an intimate acquaintance. If the world is not to be allowed into the sets, then the characters will leave the sets briefly from time to time, enter the world and describe its values, and then return to their own comfortable milieu. This light-hearted play provided the plot for the successful musical comedy *Hello, Dolly!,* which opened in 1964.

Although it makes use of the same devices, *The Skin of Our Teeth,* Wilder's last wholly new Broadway play to date, is more substantial. His starting point was James Joyce's *Finnegans Wake,* of which he has been an avid student since its publication in 1939. From this most difficult novel he took the scheme of circular action and the notion of presenting all history through the career of one family—here appropriately named Antrobus, for "all mankind." The play was first produced in 1942, World War II raged at its worst, and Wilder, then in uniform as an officer in the Army Air Corps Intelligence, could not be present for rehearsals or for the opening performance.

Much the most complex of his plays, *The Skin of Our Teeth* rests not only upon Joyce but also upon German expressionism, the music hall, burlesque, and Wilder's own earlier one-acts—an unlikely but very effective combination of forces. The title itself announces the theme, which is that no matter how hard-pressed or frightened, the human race has the power to survive its great adventure in a world where physical nature and its own internal conflicts pose endless threats. As the action proceeds, it becomes clear that the playwright holds man to be worth preserving for all his absurdity, and holds also that man's lot is worth the effort it costs him to sustain life. For this theme comedy is the proper mode, and the action is therefore designed to develop the comic possibilities of its many sources.

As he had done with *Our Town,* Wilder employed a presentational method which would permit the audience to be drawn toward the characters as individuals with private problems while recognizing that they also function as the representatives of the entire race. George and Maggie Antrobus and their servant Sabina occasionally take part in low-comedy clowning of the silent-film variety at the same time that they represent Adam, Eve, and Lilith, and, as the surname indicates, the race of man. To stress the essentially human, Wilder lets them drop their stage roles at moments and appear as actors who have been engaged to perform in a play titled *The Skin of Our Teeth*. But this is not all that they represent. Mr. Antrobus is a burlesque comedian who greets his family with epithets bordering on the obscene, and in addition he is a go-getting American businessman, rejoicing in his invention of the wheel and the alphabet, having the time of his life at a conference (of mammals), planning impatiently to rebuild his home and community after nature and warfare have demolished them. Mrs. Antrobus is the eternal homemaker and mother, cherishing her wicked son Henry (who was called Cain before he killed his brother), looking after the welfare of the race, discovering that the tomato is edible. The home of the Antrobus family stands on Cedar Street in Excelsior, New Jersey, but like the Gibbs and Webb homes of *Our Town* it also stands at the center of creation. Sabina, who represents the sensual side of man's nature, is the maid of all work, abducted from her home in the Sabine Hills. Although this complex presentation of character is not easy to manage, Wilder brings it off without confusion. In observing that the audience sees double while watching the action, he has underestimated his achievement; the keenest members of the audience will see not merely two layers of personality in each character but three, four, or even five.

To show mankind at its best, Wilder places the family in three desperate situations: the Ice Age, Noah's Flood, and a horrendous armed conflict which would seem to be his image of World War II. In the first scene Sabina appears with duster in hand like the familiar servant of a nineteenth-century drama of domestic intrigue. As the settings flap, buckle, and fly out of sight, reminding us of a worn-out tradition of theatrical production, she worries that some evil may have befallen her master, who has not yet come home. Ice is reported to be descending toward New Jersey from the north. At the end of the act the family is gathered together, along with Homer, the Muses, and Moses—all refugees—

and with the warmth provided by coffee and the burning seats of the theater, they will survive. The Flood begins when the family is attending a conference at Atlantic City; also present are representatives of all other species of mammal and, as delegates to the conference, representatives of all species of the other orders of life. When the tide rises dangerously, the family, though guilty of the seven deadly sins, is allowed to escape in a boat anchored nearby, and with them go the other creatures. Since the play is to conclude as a comedy, the members of the family when next we see them have already experienced and outlasted the third of their trials. The war which they have lived through has brought some changes. Gladys, George and Maggie's daughter, has produced an illegitimate child. Sabina has become a camp-follower. Henry, it appears, has been the enemy all along; he is the opposing self, man as his own enemy, and he is also a wild youth in rebellion against his father. But under the guidance of George—man the intellectual—the family resettles in its war-damaged home. Blackout—then Sabina reappears, duster in hand, and the play begins again, as repeatedly through endless time man strives to live in dignity.

Despite the importance of its theme, a play so defiant of convention and so severe in its demands on the analytical powers of the audience cannot please everyone. Some readers and theatergoers have taken it to be nothing more than, in Wilder's words, "a bookish fantasia about history, full of rather bloodless schoolmasterish jokes." Nevertheless the play is frequently produced. Wilder found comforting evidence of its force when shortly after the war he attended German productions in theaters provided by bombed-out churches and beer halls.

In the years since the war Wilder has continued to write, but has published less than in the first two decades of his career. His most substantial postwar works are two novels, *The Ides of March* (1948) and *The Eighth Day* (1967). Apart from a few brief essays, he provided nothing between 1948 and 1954, when *The Merchant of Yonkers* reappeared as *The Matchmaker,* though this, of course, was scarcely a new work. At the Edinburgh Festival of 1955 he offered his first completely new play in over a decade, an adaptation on existentialist lines of the *Alcestis* of Euripides titled *A Life in the Sun*. The reviews were the most condemnatory he had yet received, causing him to withdraw the work. It has since been published in a German translation as *Die Alkestiade* and has been produced in Zurich, but is unavailable in English and is unlikely to be produced again in that language. In 1957, at sixty, he returned again to the one-act play. Two short pieces, *Bernice* and *The Wreck of the 5:25*, were given in West Berlin, but were not released for performance in America and have not been published. In November of the same year *The Drunken Sisters*, a satyr play to follow *A Life in the Sun*, was printed in the *Atlantic Monthly*. An imaginative little sketch, it shows Apollo striking an agreement for the life of Admetus with the three Fates, whom he has urged to drink more than is good for them.

Still the one-act play continued to hold Wilder's interest, and in 1961 he announced a scheme to employ it on a grand scale: a double series of fourteen plays, seven on the deadly sins and seven on the ages of man. He also announced that they were not to be produced on the conventional stages of Broadway, but in an arena-style theater. Only in such a theater, he now believes, can drama regain the strength it possessed in antiquity and the Renaissance.

Early in 1962 the first three of the pieces which he wished to release were staged off-Broadway as *Plays for Bleecker Street*, the title indicating the location of the theater. Despite uneven critical notices, they drew well. *Someone from Assisi*, on the sin of lust, is the least satisfactory. It is couched in the unfortunately quaint language of the three-minute plays, and as a portrait of St. Francis in repentance for a long-forgotten sin it touches only faintly on the weaknesses of the flesh. *Infancy* and *Childhood*, on the other hand, are robust. The first reveals two adult actors dressed as children. Wheeled to the park for an outing, they pass the time in a discussion of infancy as a trying age in which parents do not comprehend, and do nothing to further, the intellectual attainments of their offspring. A subtler play, *Childhood* marks a return to the Grover's Corners mood. The three young children of a suburban couple play an elaborate game in which their parents are dead and they themselves are free to leave home. In their fantasy, a few chairs become a bus, and they board it for a cross-country trip. The father, hoping to understand their dreams, becomes the driver, and the mother queues up as another passenger. On the imaginary ride the father likens the trip to the voyage through life, since both have their dangers and pleasures. The lesson is not lost on the children, who appear, when the trip is over, to have a new consideration for their parents. But in a few minutes they are off again in another dream. The only one of the three plays to be published (in the *Atlantic Monthly* for November 1960, more than a year before the production), it is likely to have a long life.

Rich in philosophical speculation and astonishing in theatrical technique, Wilder's plays have enlivened stages throughout the world. The record of his successes stands as a denial of the frequently heard charge that the American theater lacks imagination or concerns itself only with works of obvious commercial value. If few other American playwrights as daring as Wilder have been so popular, the reason is that few others have been so skilled.

7 TENNESSEE WILLIAMS

Esther M. Jackson

When Tennessee Williams' poetic drama *The Glass Menagerie* opened in New York in 1945, a new epoch in the history of the American theater began. As Eugene O'Neill had dominated the first quarter-century of the American drama's life as an indigenous form, so Williams was to become the major figure in the second period of the theater's growth. In the twenty years or more since that first production of *The Glass Menagerie,* Williams has confirmed his position of artistic leadership in the American theater. The influence of his concept of drama, particularly that of his interpretation of character and plot, has materially affected the work of such recent playwrights as William Inge and Edward Albee. Of equal importance has been the impetus which Williams and his interpreters have given to the development of a singular dramaturgy, to the refinement of a distinctively American art of acting, staging, and designing. Of greatest significance, perhaps, has been his contribution to the development of a popular theatrical form.[1]

Williams' rise to a position of major influence in the American theater has been accompanied by an extended critical controversy. Even today, his literary form is less esteemed by such critics as John Gassner than is that of Eugene O'Neill, Thornton

[1] I wish to thank the editors of the University of Wisconsin Press for permission to include some materials which appear in my book *The Broken World of Tennessee Williams* (Madison, Wisc.: The University of Wisconsin Press, 1965).

Wilder, or Arthur Miller.[2] No single work of his has achieved the critical status won by *Mourning Becomes Electra, Our Town,* or *Death of a Salesman.* Williams is, however, particularly admired by such American critics as Gassner for the theatrical effectiveness of his work. His major asset as a dramatist is his talent for creating characters, situations, forms of dialogue, and scenic environments which possess the prized quality of verisimilitude—plausibility in performance. It is this ability to create the illusion of reality in the theater which has won for him an impressive array of honors. His first major prize was awarded in 1939 by the Group Theatre of New York. In 1940, he received one of the coveted Rockefeller Fellowships for playwriting. As early as 1944, he was cited for exceptional achievement by the National Institute of Arts and Letters. The work of his mature years has won for the playwright four New York Drama Critics' Circle Awards (1945, 1947, 1955, and 1961), two Pulitzer Prizes (1947 and 1955), and membership in the National Institute of Arts and Letters (1952).

Although he has won these tokens of acceptance from literary circles, Williams' influential position in the American theater has derived, in the main, from support of another kind. One of the most important measures of his competence has been his ability to win and to sustain the artistic loyalty of the theatrical profession. Because of the exceptional effectiveness of his plays in performance, he has been able to attract artists of extraordinary skill. Moreover, because of his commitment to the principle of artistic collaboration between playwright, director, designer, and performer, opportunities to interpret his plays are highly coveted by workers in the theater. The effect of this widespread professional admiration for Williams' sense of theatricality has been that he has had the advantage of a consistently high level of production. This excellence in production has in turn enhanced his reputation as a popular artist.

2 See, for example, John Gassner: "Homage to O'Neill," in *O'Neill and His Plays,* ed. Oscar Cargill, N. B. Fagin, and W. J. Fisher (New York: New York University Press, 1961), pp. 321–30.

Williams is perhaps the first American playwright to earn the descriptive title of "popular dramatist." [3] Certainly his work has had wider public exposure than has that of such contenders as Eugene O'Neill or the nineteenth-century dramatist Dion Boucicault. In the more than twenty years of Williams' professional career, thirteen of his plays have been produced on the New York stage.[4] His earliest professionally staged work, *Battle of Angels* (1940), was closed after a brief trial in Boston. His first professional success, *The Glass Menagerie* (1945), was followed by *A Streetcar Named Desire* (1947), *Summer and Smoke* (1948), *The Rose Tattoo* (1951), *Camino Real* (1953), *Cat on a Hot Tin Roof* (1955), *Orpheus Descending* (1957), *Garden District* (1958), *Sweet Bird of Youth* (1959), *Period of Adjustment* (1960), *The Night of the Iguana* (1962), and *The Milk Train Doesn't Stop Here Anymore* (1963). *You Touched Me,* written in collaboration with Donald Windham, was produced in 1945. Williams' success as popular artist has not, however, been confined to the New York stage. Four of his major works, *The Glass Menagerie,*

[3] Eugene O'Neill has a longer list of produced plays, some thirty-eight, including posthumously produced works, such as *Long Day's Journey into Night, A Touch of the Poet,* and *Hughie.* The Irish-American dramatist Dion Boucicault (1822–1890) wrote one hundred fifty plays. However, neither of these rival dramatists has had the exposure which Williams' works have gained. A major factor in this difference is the motion-picture market. Williams has in addition a growing audience in other parts of the world. His literary agent reports that permissions to produce *A Streetcar Named Desire* have already been granted in thirty-six countries in Europe, Asia, and Africa.

[4] Since this chapter was written, Williams has had a fourteenth New York opening. *Slapstick Tragedy,* a bill composed of two one-act plays, *The Mutilated* and *The Gnadiges Fräulein,* opened for a brief run at the Longacre Theatre on February 26, 1966.

Williams' list of New York revivals has also lengthened. *The Rose Tattoo* opened to highly favorable reviews at the City Center of Music and Drama on October 20, 1966. Other successful revivals have included the production of *Summer and Smoke* at Circle-in-the-Square, March, 1952; *Camino Real* at the St. Marks Playhouse, May, 1960; and *The Glass Menagerie* at the Brooks Atkinson Theatre, May, 1965.

Somewhat less successful were the productions of *A Streetcar Named Desire* at the City Center in February, 1956, and *The Milk Train Doesn't Stop Here Anymore* at the Brooks Atkinson Theatre in January, 1964.

A Streetcar Named Desire, Summer and Smoke, and *Cat on a Hot Tin Roof,* have been widely performed by educational, community, and professional theater companies throughout the United States. *Educational Theatre Journal,* in a series of articles on play-selection in American colleges and universities, records that the modern play most frequently produced in the period between 1955 and 1960 was *The Glass Menagerie.*[5]

Although Williams is regarded primarily as a writer for the stage, it is possible that his most effective medium of popularization has been the motion picture. His emphasis on visual spectacle has provided a viable base for the transposition of his works into the cinematic medium. To date, ten of his full-length plays have been adapted for motion-picture audiences: *The Glass Menagerie* (1950), *A Streetcar Named Desire* (1952), *The Rose Tattoo* (1956), *Cat on a Hot Tin Roof* (1958), *Orpheus Descending* (retitled *The Fugitive Kind,* 1960), *Suddenly Last Summer* (from *Garden District;* 1960), *Summer and Smoke* (1962), *Sweet Bird of Youth* (1962), *Period of Adjustment* (1962), and *The Night of the Iguana* (1964). An eleventh film, *Baby Doll* (1956), was composed by director Elia Kazan from two early works—*Baby Doll,* from the collection *27 Wagons Full of Cotton,* and *The Unsatisfactory Supper,* from the anthology *American Blues.*[6]

But Williams is a popular playwright not only in terms of his success as a commercial artist but also by reason of dramatic intent. Indeed, the controversy which has attended his career may be traced in large measure to his attempt to recover the natural function of the drama as the mirror of popular imagination. Although he shares many of the concerns of a larger group of contemporary dramatists, his theater is not in the literary tradition established by such playwrights as Luigi Pirandello, Bertolt Brecht, Jean Giraudoux, Jean-Paul Sartre, T. S. Eliot, and

[5] See, for example, Theodore Shank's report in *The Educational Theatre Journal,* XIII: 2 (May 1961), 113.

[6] *The Roman Spring of Mrs. Stone,* a film based on Williams' novel of the same name, was released in 1961. *This Property Is Condemned,* an expanded version of a one-act play from the series *27 Wagons Full of Cotton,* was released in 1966.

Thornton Wilder. On the contrary, Williams attempts to recover for drama its primary identity as a pre-literary form. He is committed to a theater that is extraverbal in nature, to a dramatic form that seeks to explore not only rational but also irrational and suprarational planes of human experience. Williams proposes to mirror the ambiguous reality of his perception in a language which can be understood by popular audiences. He undertakes to project those events, ideas, attitudes, and collective feelings that characterize life in the mid-twentieth century into the physical, emotional, moral, and symbolic environment of the common man. He writes of this motive in the preface to *The Glass Menagerie:* "These remarks are not meant as a preface only to this particular play. They have to do with a conception of a new, plastic theatre which must take the place of the exhausted theatre of realistic conventions if the theatre is to resume vitality as a part of our culture." [7]

For Williams, vitality means the return of the drama to joyous and irreverent entertainment, to the simulation of shock and terror, and to the ritual exploration of modern man's life cycle. In order to revitalize theater, he proposes—as have other popular playwrights in the past—the modification of conventional drama through the introduction of idiomatic forms drawn from the vulgar arts. *The Glass Menagerie, A Streetcar Named Desire,* and *Cat on a Hot Tin Roof* gain much of their popular appeal from familiar elements adapted from the cinema, radio, and television, from American jazz music and folk songs, from circuses, political rallies, and revivals, and from the common language of the American streets. Williams describes his linguistic method in the early play *Ten Blocks on the Camino Real:* "I am trying to catch the quality of really 'tough' Americana of the comic sheets . . . . all the rootless, unstable and highly spirited life beneath the middle-class social level in the States." [8]

[7] Tennessee Williams: Introduction to *The Glass Managerie* (New York: Random House, 1945), p. ix.

[8] Tennessee Williams: *Ten Blocks on the Camino Real* in *American Blues* (New York: Dramatists Play Service, 1948), Block VII, p. 58.

Williams' anti-traditional approach to drama is not accidental. On the contrary, it represents a conscious effort to mirror new perceptions of reality. The playwright's seeming lack of regard for the Aristotelian imperatives—unity of plot, nobility of character, refinement of language, control of violence, and subordination of spectacle—is but the reflection of his attempt to create a form which is true to the realities of our time. Williams' interest in a popular form is certainly not unique in the annals of American theater. Indeed, the brief history of the American drama has been the record of a continuous search for a popular form. The American playwrights of the late-eighteenth and nineteenth centuries introduced native characters and contemporary themes into traditional European forms. In the twentieth century the drive toward the creation of a popular American drama gained momentum in the pioneering work of Eugene O'Neill. The plays of Elmer Rice, Clifford Odets, Paul Green, Thornton Wilder, and Arthur Miller have built upon O'Neill's idea of a "grassroots" theater.

Williams' plays about contemporary life differ from those of more orthodox writers such as O'Neill, Wilder, and Miller. For Williams' dramas are not simply written *about* common people, they are designed *for* common people. Only two of his long plays are written in a way which excludes large numbers of American spectators from the full appreciation of their contents. *Camino Real* and *The Milk Train Doesn't Stop Here Anymore* have many of the intellectual prerequisites which limit wide public involvement in plays such as *The Hairy Ape, Mourning Becomes Electra,* and *The Skin of Our Teeth.* Like these earlier works, *Camino Real* and *The Milk Train Doesn't Stop Here Anymore* obscure some of their contents beneath complex literary myths. In the main, however, Williams' works have profited from his popular view of drama as a sensuous rather than a rational form. For this view has allowed him to interpret human conflict in a syntax which is universal; that is, in a richly symbolic language which links word to gesture, movement, music, sound, design, and poetic inference.

Williams' success in rendering theatrical images in a popular language is not entirely the result of personal gifts. Certainly, he has had advantages which were not fully accessible to earlier playwrights. Out of the experimentation of O'Neill, Wilder, Odets, Elmer Rice, William Saroyan, and others, there had developed by 1945 a kind of American theatrical language: a system of communication with its own themes, types of character, modes of speech, styles of acting, and patterns of staging. This poetic language had a parallel in an emerging art of the *mise-en-scène,* an art of production which had been given impetus in the twenties by O'Neill and the members of the Provincetown group.

During the course of the thirties and forties, this new American dramaturgy had been undergirded by the formulation of a significant body of dramatic theory. Williams, like others among the second generation of American playwrights of the twentieth century, inherited the basic communicative structure on which his own linguistic system was to be built. He seems to have learned the rudiments of this theatrical syntax in several academic settings: at the University of Missouri, at St. Louis's Washington University, at the State University of Iowa, and—later—at New York's New School for Social Research. He gained from the university setting an aesthetic and literary orientation which was to support his own theory of form. But more important was the fact that he acquired technical skill in the use of a conventional language common to the entire range of activities which characterized the developing American theater.

But if Williams gained technical skill and literary background in the university, he acquired a practical understanding of the drama in the theater itself. Like Molière, he put together his controversial concept of form under the influence of a young and gifted provincial company. In the introduction to *27 Wagons Full of Cotton,* he has written of his apprenticeship with "The Mummers" of St. Louis, Missouri:

> The Mummers of St. Louis were my professional youth. They were the disorderly theater group of St. Louis, standing socially, if not also artistically, opposite to the usual Little Theater

group. . . . Dynamism was what The Mummers had and for about five years—roughly from about 1935 to 1940—they burned like one of Miss Millay's improvident little candles—and then expired. . . . They put on bad shows sometimes, but they never put on a show that didn't deliver a punch to the solar plexus, maybe not in the first act, maybe not in the second, but always at last a good hard punch was delivered, and it made a difference in the lives of the spectators that they had come to that place and seen that show.[9]

It was, apparently, during this period of practical apprenticeship that Williams developed his concept of a popular American form. The short plays of the collections 27 *Wagons Full of Cotton* and *American Blues* give some idea as to the level of maturity to which this concept had developed by 1940. In this early period, he seems to have experimented with other kinds of writing. Some of the short stories written during this time have been published in the collections *One Arm* (1948) and *Hard Candy* (1954). Examples of his early poetry may be seen in the volume *In the Winter of Cities* (1956) and in the New Directions series Volumes XI, XII, and XIII. Plays, stories, and verse appear to have been a part of his broad experimentation with the problem of creating an effective language for his popular theater.

In his continuing attempt to develop a popular form, Williams seems to have sought permanent ties with practical theater. After his departure from St. Louis, he established new relationships with the professional world of directors, designers, and actors. During the early years of his New York career, he was associated with the gifted director of the Dallas Theatre, Margo Jones. It was Miss Jones who assisted Eddie Dowling in the staging of *The Glass Menagerie*. Later, she was to direct both the Dallas and New York productions of *Summer and Smoke*. In the years that followed, Williams' plays were staged by other talented directors

[9] Tennessee Williams: Introduction to 27 *Wagons Full of Cotton* (Norfolk, Conn.: New Directions, 1946), pp. viii–x.

in the New York theater—Daniel Mann, Harold Clurman, José Quintero, Herbert Machiz, George Roy Hill, and Frank Corsaro. Perhaps the most significant association of his professional career was that which involved Elia Kazan. Between 1947 and 1960, Kazan staged four plays of Williams' major period: *A Streetcar Named Desire, Camino Real, Cat on a Hot Tin Roof,* and *Sweet Bird of Youth.* In addition, he directed two films, *A Streetcar Named Desire* and *Baby Doll.* In the circle composed of Kazan, the designer Jo Mielziner, the teacher and theorist Lee Strasberg, and the associates of Actors Studio, Williams found an important factor in the widening success of his middle period. For out of this creative association there emerged a mature dramaturgy for his theater, an art of acting, directing, and designing appropriate to the demands of his texts.

To date, Williams' dramatic form seems to have passed through three significant stages of development. The playwright has described the first of these as "personal lyricism." The plays written before 1945 are concerned with the essentially poetic problems of self-expression, self-identification, and even self-creation. The most mature example of this early expressive form is *The Glass Menagerie.* This work, like the short plays that precede it, represents an attempt to re-create a singularly lyric vision of reality. Williams projects upon the stage—the symbolic "screen" of consciousness—all of the shapes, sounds, colors, textures, and moods that characterize the protagonist's memory of the past. He symbolizes his vision of this reality in the metaphor "The Glass Menagerie." But Williams' vision is not merely an illusion reinvoked for the delight of the spectator. Like the Proustian hero, his poet-figure Tom seeks to discover within the sensuous fabric of experience the form of absolute truth. Williams thus introduces into his popular theater a theme which has also had treatment in the work of such contemporary European dramatists as Luigi Pirandello, Jean-Paul Sartre, and Albert Camus. What is the relationship of experience to reality? In this early play, Williams does not offer a conclusive answer to the question but rather attempts to isolate the alternative truths which emerge as his spectacle unfolds. The poet-figure Tom identifies four possibilities about existence: the truth of action, the truth of ideals, the truth of beauty, and the contemplative truth of art.

In the second phase of his work—a phase commonly regarded as the major period of his achievement—Williams attempts to extend the range of meaning affecting his lyric search for truth. In the preface to *Cat on a Hot Tin Roof,* he writes that he wishes to objectify the personal vision which is the basis of his lyric form. There emerges in the plays written between 1945 and 1955 a second level of interpretation. In the plays of this middle period, Williams attempts to create a popular myth out of contents drawn from common experience. He borrows elements of his symbolic structure from Christian theology, Greek mythology, Freudian psychology, and from the cultural history of the United States, particularly that of the rural South. *A Streetcar Named Desire, Summer and Smoke, Camino Real,* and *Cat on a Hot Tin Roof* have as their first level of interpretation the lyric form of self-exploration and self-expression. But in addition, Williams offers a more objective level of interpretation through the medium of his synthetic myth.

Perhaps the most ambitious of Williams' efforts in the construction of a modern myth is *Camino Real.* Here he uses the popular legend of the American soldier Kilroy to dramatize the threat of human annihilation in our time. Williams sets his play in a small town in Central America, but through the use of his mythic structure, he is able to draw correspondences between the problems of the twentieth century and those of earlier epochs in human history. In *Streetcar, Summer and Smoke, Cat on a Hot Tin Roof,* and *Camino Real,* Williams attempts to help the American spectator to interpret his personal crises by providing him with mythic reference to persistent patterns in the history of mankind.

In the plays written since 1955, Williams has attempted to resolve his contemporary reading of recurrent life patterns. *Orpheus Descending, Suddenly Last Summer, Sweet Bird of Youth,*

The Night of the Iguana, and *The Milk Train Doesn't Stop Here Anymore* are notable for the presence of a tentative resolution of human conflict. The fragmentary cycle of such early plays as *The Glass Menagerie* is gradually submerged in a pattern that is essentially theological in nature. It is consistent with Williams' dramatic intent that the proposition which he offers for human salvation should be relevant to the experience of the common man. It is not surprising, in the context of this intent, that Williams should offer God as the answer to the problem of human suffering. That it is God whom his protagonist seeks becomes quite clear in such late works as *Suddenly Last Summer, The Night of the Iguana,* and *The Milk Train.* This theological motive, barely suggested by Blanche in *Streetcar,* is openly embraced by Shannon, the protagonist of *Night of the Iguana.* The dramatic conclusion which Williams reaches in his late works is essentially that offered by more orthodox dramatists, such as T. S. Eliot and Archibald MacLeish. However, Williams differs from Eliot and Mac-Leish in the image of God which he creates. For Williams' God is not the philosophical abstraction of *The Cocktail Party,* nor is he the inscrutable Old Testament deity of *J.B.* Williams' God, like his man, is the figment of the popular imagination. He is the stern but forgiving "Father" of American Protestantism.

Tennessee Williams' position as the leading popular dramatist in the American theater may be attributed to a number of interrelated factors. Like other major contemporary writers, he attempts to create for modern man an image of his urgent concerns. But Williams has a significant advantage over other American dramatists in his ability to translate the particulars of the emotional, social, and moral issues of the time into a common language of great power. As in the past, the talent for dramatizing in the language of the common man the political events, philosophical perceptions, and social conditions of an age has brought to the playwright and his theater a wide and varied audience. While we cannot be assured that Williams' plays will endure as examples of great drama, it seems certain that he will remain a significant figure in the history of the American theater. Popular playwrights in years to come will remain indebted to his skill as a mediator between past and present, tradition and originality, the theater and the common man.

8 ARTHUR MILLER

Gerald Weales

*And the Lord said unto Moses
in Midian, Go, return into Egypt.*

In 1964, after an eight-year exile in a Midian a great deal less comfortable than that of Moses, Arthur Miller returned to the New York stage. Within a year, he and the Lincoln Center Repertory Theater offered two new plays—*After the Fall* and *Incident at Vichy*. The first of these is an excessively long self-analysis by a character whose biography so much resembles the playwright's that most critics take it as Miller's *Long Day's Journey into Night*. The second is a kind of round-table discussion over a grave, an incident—as the title says—in which one man finds the power to act. Although they are very different in superficial ways, the plays are alike in theme and tone. It is the second of these— the tone—which justifies the biblical quotation with which I have opened this essay. Miller has returned to the stage dressed in prophetic robes, clothed in a ponderousness that his early plays usually escaped. It is as though he came back not as *a* playwright, but as *The* Playwright—with a capital letter, an image of eminence, a sense of his own high seriousness and his duty as an artist. But this is being unfair to the new Miller. He has always taken himself seriously as an artist, and he has always taken seriously the artist's function in society. If the new plays are inferior to the

Some of the material on the early plays of Miller appeared earlier in Gerald Weales, *American Drama Since World War II* (New York: Harcour, Brace & World, 1962).

early ones—and I think they are—their shortcomings can best be
seen in recognizing that there is not a complete break between
early and late Miller. There are similarities in idea, in technique,
in language. To understand what is new in the most recent
Miller, it is best to look at his work as a whole, to attempt to understand what he has wanted to say and how he has tried to say it
from the beginning.

Compared with most American playwrights, Miller has written
a great deal about his work and how it is to be taken. If his
speeches, essays, and introductions were collected, they might
look skimpy alongside Bertolt Brecht's theoretical writings, but
they would form a respectable volume—one, incidentally, in
which aesthetics would share space with apologetics and insight
would elbow obscurity. Among the most important of his essays
is the one called "On Social Plays," which served as an introduction to the 1955 edition of *A View from the Bridge*. Although there is a kind of vagueness about the essay, as there is
about so much of Miller's critical writing, it does make clear that
he believes that the serious playwright must write social drama.
For him, however, the genre is not simply "an arraignment of
society's evils." The true social drama, which he calls the "Whole
Drama," must recognize that man has both a subjective and an
objective existence, that he belongs not only to himself and his
family but to the world beyond. This definition fits the four plays
that made Miller famous—*All My Sons* (1947), *Death of a Salesman* (1949), *The Crucible* (1953), and *A View from the Bridge*
(1955). With a shift in emphasis, it also fits the two plays produced in 1964.

If a playwright is to be concerned with both psychological man
and social man, as Miller's definition of social drama says he
must, he is inevitably forced to deal with the problem of identity.
This is what Miller has always written about, and it is as clearly
the subject of *Incident at Vichy* as it is of *All My Sons*. In Miller's
early work, each of his heroes is involved in a struggle which results from his acceptance or his rejection of an image of himself—
an image that grows out of the values and the prejudices of his

society. That society may be as narrow as Eddie Carbone's neighborhood in *A View from the Bridge* or as wide as the contemporary America that helped form the Willy Loman we meet in *Death of a Salesman*. Although this preoccupation may be found in most of Miller's short stories, in his novel *Focus,* and in his very early plays, it can be seen most clearly where it is most effectively presented—in his major plays, beginning with *All My Sons*. The hero of that play, Joe Keller, is a case in point. He is a good husband and a good father, but he fails to be the good man, the good citizen that his son Chris demands. Near the end of the play, Joe cries out: "I'm his father and he's my son, and if there's something bigger than that I'll put a bullet in my head!" When Chris, now dead, convinces him through a letter that there is something bigger, that his guilt in shipping out faulty airplane parts cannot be excused by his desire to save the family business, Joe does commit suicide. His death, however, is more than a single man's punishment, for Joe Keller is a product of his society. He not only accepts the American myth of the privacy of the family, but he has adopted as a working instrument the familiar attitude that there is a difference between morality and business ethics. Joe Keller is a self-made man, an image of American success, who is destroyed when he is forced to see that image in another context —through the eyes of his idealist son.

After the narrow didacticism of *All My Sons,* Miller went on to write, in *Death of a Salesman,* a play in which the social implications are so firmly enmeshed in the psychological make-up of his hero that it is never possible to reduce Willy's pathetic death to social criticism. When we meet Willy, he, like Joe Keller, is past the point of choice. From the conflicting success images that wander through his troubled brain comes Willy's double ambition— to be rich and to be loved. As he tells Ben: "the wonder of this country [is] that a man can end with diamonds here on the basis of being liked!" Willy's faith in the magic of "personal attractiveness" as a way to success carries him beyond cause and effect to necessity; he assumes that success falls inevitably to the man with the right smile, the best line, the most charm—the man who is not only liked, but "well liked." He has completely embraced the American myth, born of the advertisers, that promises us love and a fortune as soon as we clear up our pimples, stop underarm perspiration, learn to play the piano; for this reason, the brand names that turn up in Willy's speeches are more than narrow realism. He regularly confuses labels with reality. In his last scene with his son Biff, Willy cries out: "I am not a dime a dozen! I am Willy Loman, and you are Biff Loman!" The strength and the pathos of that cry lie in the fact that Willy still thinks that the name should mean something; it is effective within the play because we have heard him imply that a punching bag is good because, as he says, "It's got Gene Tunney's signature on it."

The distance between the actual Willy and the Willy as image is so great when the play opens that he can no longer lie to himself with conviction; what the play gives us is the final disintegration of a man who has never even approached his idea of what by rights he ought to have been. His ideal may have been the old salesman, who at the age of eighty-four could, through the strength of personality, sit in a hotel room and command buyers; but his model is that American mythic figure, the traveling salesman of the dirty joke. Willy shares his culture's conviction that personality is a matter of mannerism and in the sharing develops a style that is compounded of falseness, the mock assurance of what his son Happy calls "the old humor, the old confidence." His act, however, is as much for himself as it is for his customers. The play shows quite clearly that from the beginning of his career Willy has lied about the size of his sales, the warmth of his reception, the number of his friends. It is true that he occasionally doubts himself, but usually he rationalizes his failure. His continuing self-delusion and his occasional self-awareness serve the same purpose; they keep him from questioning the assumptions that lie beneath his failure and his pretense of success.

By the time we get to him, his struggle to hold on to his dream has become so intense that all control is gone. Past and present have become one, and so have fact and fiction. When Biff tries to give him peace by making him realize that there is no crime in being a failure and a mediocrity, Willy hears only what he wants to hear. He takes Biff's tears not only as an evidence of love, which they are, but as a kind of testimonial, an assurance that Willy's way has been the right one all along. Once again secure in his dream, Willy goes to his suicide's death, convinced that when Biff gets the insurance money, "that boy is going to be magnificent." The play is not a simple rejection of Willy's dream. Since Willy has spent his life trying to fit himself into one of the pigeonholes of our society and since Biff is so much like Willy, the final irony of the play may lie in Biff's end-of-the-play declaration, "I know who I am, kid."

Joe Keller and Willy Loman are both consenting victims, men who attach themselves to images which their society has created and called good. The hero of Miller's next play, *The Crucible,* refuses to accept the label that his society tries to force on him. John Proctor dies at the end—and his society kills him—but his death is a romantic one, a kind of triumph, an affirmation of the individual. It may be that Proctor's decision to hang rather than to confess grew out of Miller's involvement in the immediate political situation from which *The Crucible* was drawn. It was the McCarthy era, when so many writers and performers—moved by fear or economic necessity or a genuine break with their ideological past—stepped forward to confess their political sins and to name their fellow sinners. Under such circumstances, it is hardly surprising that Miller chose a hero who could say *no.* And yet the playwright was not interested in a simple propaganda play.

The materials for such a play are there—the hysteria-ridden community, the corrupt accusers, the innocent good people willing to die for their principles. With John Proctor, however, Miller goes for something deeper than the one-dimensional "good guy." Proctor is enough a product of his society to think of himself as a sinner for having slept with Abigail Williams; so he carries a burden of guilt before he is charged with having consorted with the devil. When he is finally faced with the choice of death or confession, his guilt as an adulterer becomes confused with his innocence as a witch; one sin against society comes to look like another. The stage is set for another victim-hero, for a John Proctor who is willing to be what men say he is, but at the last minute he chooses to be his own man. "How may I live without my name?" he asks and, finding no answer, he tears up his confession and goes to the gallows.

Eddie Carbone in *A View from the Bridge* also dies crying out for his name, but he is asking for a lie that will let him live or, failing that, for death. Eddie is like Joe Keller and Willy Loman in that he accepts the rules of his society, an Italian neighborhood in Brooklyn, but he dies because he violates them. Miller wants us to believe that Eddie informs on Rodolpho, an illegal immigrant, because he is driven by a passion as powerful and as impersonal as fate. The interesting thing about Eddie is not the passion that pushes him, but his refusal to recognize it for what it is. He gets rid of Rodolpho not so much out of jealousy, but because the boy's presence nags at him, almost forces him to put a label on his incestuous love for his niece and his homosexual attraction to the boy himself. It is almost as though he becomes an *informer* to keep from wearing some name still more terrible to him. He cannot live under the lesser label either, so he moves into battle with the avenging brother Marco, demanding, "Gimme my name."

Each of these plays has a personality of its own, an action and an intention that separates it from the other three, but all of them are variations on the same theme. The basic premise of all four is that society is an image-making machine, a purveyor of myths and prejudices which provide the false faces and false values which modern man wears. The implication is that the individual has little choice—that he can conform and be destroyed, as Joe Keller and Willy Loman are, or that he can refuse to conform and be destroyed, as John Proctor and Eddie Carbone are. Despite the blackness of this description, the plays are not pessimistic, because inherent in them is a kind of vague faith in man, a suspicion that the individual may finally be able to retain his integrity. This possibility appears, most conventionally, in the platitudes of Chris, the avenging idealist of *All My Sons,* and in the kind of death John Proctor dies in *The Crucible.* In *A View from the Bridge* it lies outside the action of the play, in Miller's attempt, speaking through the narrator Alfieri, to engraft a ritual purity on Eddie: "not purely good, but himself purely."

If the possibility appears at all in *Death of a Salesman*—and I think it does—it does not lie in the possible right choice implied by Biff's "He had the wrong dreams." It certainly does not lie in Biff himself, in all those references to working with the hands, nor in the alternative suggested by Charley and Bernard. It is in Willy's vitality, in his perverse commitment to a pointless dream, in his inability simply to walk away. This last phrase, of course, is a paraphrase of one of Miller's unnecessary attempts to define tragedy. What I'm saying about *Death of a Salesman,* I suppose, is that Willy Loman is a character so complex, so contradictory, so vulnerable, so insensitive, so trusting, so distrustful, so blind, so aware—in short, so human—that he forces man on us by being one.

A few years after these plays were written, Miller tried to give a positive name to whatever it was in man that was going to save him. He had tried before in *Situation Normal,* the book he wrote during the war, but the best he could come up with then was: "And that Belief says, simply, that we believe all men are equal." In the late 1950's he succumbed to the bromide of the decade and began to talk about love. In the introduction to the *Collected Plays,* he added an ex-post-facto alternative to *Death of a Salesman* by suggesting that Biff represents a "system of love" that can oppose Willy's "law of success." In "Bridge to a Savage World," an *Esquire* article containing material that was to go into a film on juvenile delinquency, Miller speaks of "the measure of love which we must bring to our lives if we are not to slide back into a life of violence." [1] Finally, in *The Misfits,* his 1961 film, he lets his hero and heroine, like a William Inge couple, follow "that big star straight on" to find their way home in the dark. Brotherhood and love, however admirable, are a bit amorphous divorced from a specific doctrine—religious, political, or psychological. The terms might have some meaning in a particular situation (if it is

[1] Arthur Miller, "Bridge to a Savage World," *Esquire,* October 1958, 185–190.

not a literary cliché, like the end of *The Misfits*), but it is always difficult to extrapolate from a momentary experience to find a general principle by which man can live. That I assume is what Quentin means in *After the Fall* when he says forlornly: "Socialism once, then love; some final hope is gone that always saved before the end!"

Despite Quentin's statement of loss, *After the Fall* ends in a positive act, and so does *Incident at Vichy*. Quentin goes to meet Holga, ready to commit himself once again to a personal relationship—which we are to take as a commitment to life. The Prince in *Incident at Vichy* gives up the pass that would free him to save Leduc's life. Despite these acts, however, the two new plays are a great deal more somber than the early Miller plays. The difference is a philosophic one, or would be if the early plays were as formal in their point of view as the new ones are. The difference lies in the way Miller uses the problem of identity. I do not mean that he has ceased to accept that men have images forced upon them. One of the lines of action in *Incident at Vichy*—although it might be called *a line of inaction*—has to do with the failure of the waiting men to resist what is being done to them. A great deal of the discussion has to do with how one should act in the face of his destroyers, what role he should play in an attempt to save himself. The implication is that their failure to agree to attack the guard is their way of consenting to their own destruction. Lebeau, the painter, admits that he feels guilty although he knows he has done nothing wrong and he is not ashamed of being a Jew. Yet, he can say: "Maybe it's that they keep saying such terrible things about us, and you can't answer." It is Leduc, the psychiatrist, who states the proposition formally: "So that one way or the other, with illusions or without them, exhausted or fresh—we have been trained to die." Although there is a relationship between this kind of thinking and the conception of Willy Loman as a man attempting to be the success his society admires, there is a great difference too. Willy, as a consenting victim, is a product of Miller's observation; the consenting victims of *Incident at Vichy* are products turned out on the Bruno Bettelheim–Hannah Arendt line—explanations of totalitarian success which almost become apologies for it.

There is, then, a qualitative difference between the conceptions of society in *Death of a Salesman* and in *Incident at Vichy*. That difference, however, is not apparent if we look at *After the Fall* alongside *Salesman*. The pressures that beset Quentin and his friends and relatives are not necessarily the same ones that push Willy around, but they are the same kind. It is clear in *After the Fall* that much of Maggie's behavior is the result of her doing what is expected of her, and that Louise sees herself and Quentin in the roles that her psychoanalysis insists that they play. In the political subplot, Mickey testifies and names names partly because his new affluence requires that he should, and Lou, who makes a John Proctor-refusal, admits that in the past he has compromised his sense of his own honesty, tailored himself to fit Party requirements.

Yet *After the Fall* and *Incident at Vichy* are thematically two of a kind. The real split between these two plays and the earlier ones can be found in what the heroes are looking for—or, at least, in what they find. Like John Proctor and Eddie Carbone, both Quentin and Von Berg are concerned about their names. When Leduc seems surprised that Von Berg should take his title seriously, the Prince answers: "It is not a 'title'; it is my name, my family." Since he goes on to use words like *dishonor,* one might assume that *name* has the same value here as it does in *A View from the Bridge* or *The Crucible*. At this point in the play, it may have such value, at least for Von Berg, but the lesson that the play is going to teach him is to understand *name* as Quentin uses it when he keeps asking over and over in whose name one turns one's back. In the early Miller plays the quest for identity, for name, was a search for integrity. In *After the Fall* and *Incident at Vichy* that quest has become an attempt to find a workable definition.

In *After the Fall*, Quentin is faced with the problem of coming to some conclusion about himself which will make it possible for him to operate in the world. He is attracted to Holga, but he hesitates to commit himself to her, because so many of the commitments of his past—personal, political, and professional—have collapsed, leaving him nothing. The play is Quentin's look at that past, his attempt to find meaning in it. Early in the play, he says sadly: "I feel . . . unblessed." He is bothered throughout the play by a girl named Felice, whom he cannot get out of his mind. Once, casually, he did something that changed the course of her life, and he continually sees her, her hand lifted in benediction, saying: "I'll always bless you." At the end of the play, when he faces the figures from his past, like the director in Fellini's $8\frac{1}{2}$, he stops Felice from lifting her hand. He accepts that he is unblessed. What he learns in the course of the play is that he has spent his life trying, one way or another, to establish his innocence. The guilt that he feels about the way he has treated his family, about his two failed marriages, about his reluctance to defend his old friend has always been transferred to the other person in the relationship. At the end, he accepts that it is after the fall, that there is no innocence, that the guilt is his. Earlier in the play Holga tells him her recurrent dream. In it she has an idiot child, which she knows represents her life; she wants to run away from it, but she stays and finally she brings herself to kiss it. In case Quentin or the audience has missed the point of the dream, she adds the moral: "I think one must finally take one's life in one's arms, Quentin."

Accepting one's life—at least in the context of *After the Fall*—is more complicated than simply recognizing that any relationship implies responsibilities on both sides. The guilt that Quentin assumes is something very like original sin: an acceptance that he—and all men—are evil. Or that they have evil in them—the capacity to kill. This is presented several ways in the play. Verbally, in Quentin's statements about his failure to grieve for his dead—for Lou, for his mother, for Maggie—visually, in the scene in which he begins to strangle Maggie and finds himself strangling his mother; metaphorically, in the concentration-camp tower that broods over the whole play. This is the element in the play that is most difficult to take, but it is a necessary part of the idea Miller has imposed on his play. Toward the end of the play, Quentin turns toward the tower and says: "My brothers died here . . ." and then, looking down at Maggie lying at his feet, goes on ". . . but my brothers built this place." What is finally being said in *After the Fall* is not that Quentin's life shows him capable of cruelty, of murder even, but that he must accept his complicity in all the evil in the world. Holga, who carries the messages for Miller, says: ". . . no one they didn't kill can be innocent again."

Incident at Vichy comes to the same conclusion. In this instance it is not self-examination that brings self-knowledge to Von Berg; it is a lesson forced on him from outside by Leduc, who from the beginning of the play has accepted that man is inherently evil. When he remarks that he believes the rumor that there are furnaces waiting to destroy them all, it is not because the destroyers are Germans or Nazis, but "It's exactly because they are people that I speak this way." Von Berg, on the other hand, believes that there are "certain people," not identifiable by race or class, through whom all that is best in civilization will finally survive. He imagines that his sympathy for the suffering of the Jews separates him from their tormentors. He is so horrified by what has happened in his native Austria that he has, as he says, "put a pistol to my head!" But he has not pulled the trigger and, as Holga points out in *After the Fall,* by being alive he fails to be innocent. Leduc reminds him that the cousin he mentions early in the play, a man for whom he obviously has some affection, is a Nazi. "It's not your guilt I want," says Leduc, "it's your responsibility."

That statement, however, is false—if not for Leduc, certainly for Miller. What he wants in this play is for Von Berg to recognize his guilt, as Quentin accepts his in *After the Fall.* In an article in *The New York Times Magazine*[2] Miller set out to correct some misconceptions that he felt had grown up around *Incident at Vichy.* He makes quite clear that, to him, the story is relatively unimportant and that Von Berg's heroic act at the end is gratui-

[2] Arthur Miller, "Our Guilt for the World's Evil," *The New York Times Magazine,* January 3, 1965, pp. 10–11, 48.

tous. "The first problem is not what to do about it," he says, "but to discover our own relationship to evil, its reflection of ourselves." If Quentin is a usable analogy for Miller himself, it would seem that the events of the eight years before the writing of *Vichy* made Miller find in himself qualities that he can accept only with difficulty. The accepting becomes possible, however, by extending the *mea culpa* to take in all men. He chooses to do this by embracing the commonplaces of contemporary psychology, but —since he is still a social dramatist—he uses the complicity gambit to turn personal guilt into public guilt. What this means to Miller as a playwright is that he no longer deals with man's struggle against the images being forced on him; instead, he becomes an image-forcer himself. After all the identity searching, the name that Quentin and Von Berg end up with is Everyman as Executioner. Both plays suggest—insist really—that once this label is accepted, once the illusion of innocence is pushed aside, a man is free to act—even to act as a lover (like Quentin) or a martyr (like Von Berg). These positive acts, however, are simply the residue left by the burning away of the naïve belief in man implicit in the early plays. In *After the Fall* and *Incident at Vichy*, the heroes are not in a struggle; they are in analysis. The analysis is successful when they accept that they fit the love-hate stereotype of the psychological man.

At the beginning of this chapter, I said that *Fall* and *Vichy* are inferior to the earlier plays. Although what Miller has to say in the new plays is philosophically suspect, it is not his theme but his commitment to it that has crippled his work. His new truth is not an impetus to creativity, but a doctrine that must be illustrated. In the past, he has occasionally been criticized for his didacticism, but in none of the early plays, not even in *All My Sons* and *The Crucible,* has he sacrificed action to argument. There are defects enough in the early plays—the hidden-letter trick in *All My Sons,* Elizabeth's loving lie in *The Crucible*—defects that grow out of a need to let the action make a social point. Still, his main characters—even John Proctor—are more than one-dimensional vehicles. All the early plays are attempts to understand man and his society by confronting a particular man with a particular situation. The generalizations to be made from that particularity lie outside the play—with the audience, with the critic, with the playwright in his theoretical writings. In the new plays, the situations and the characters are only demonstration models. The playwright has moved from the creation of character to the making of statements, from the concrete to the abstract. This can best be seen if we look at *After the Fall* alongside *Death of a Salesman,* the early play that it most resembles.

The first title for *Salesman* was *The Inside of His Head,* which would suit *After the Fall* just as well. According to the first stage direction of *Fall:* "The action takes place in the mind, thought, and memory of Quentin." Although the version of *Salesman* that finally reached the stage has objective scenes as well as subjective ones, both *Salesman* and *After the Fall* make use of the ideas and the devices of expressionistic theater. The barriers of time and space disappear. The skeletal set of *Salesman* and the free-form set of *Fall* were conceived to let Miller's heroes step freely from the present to the past, or, particularly in the case of Quentin, from one moment in the past to another. Both plays are designed, then, to let the playwright (and his characters) escape the restrictions of conventional realism. The difference between the two plays lies in the way the playwright uses his freedom. In *Salesman* we follow Willy through the last desperate day of his existence, watching him clutch at impossible and mostly imaginary straws, until, through Biff, he is able to find the release that will let him die. The jumble of memories that nag at him are not simply explanatory flashbacks, although there is exposition in them. Since they are as real to Willy as the immediate events, they contribute to his disintegration. In *Salesman,* then, all the scenes are part of the play's action. In *After the Fall* this is hardly the case. What happens in that play is that Quentin decides to go meet Holga at the airport; the action, presumably, is his process of reaching that decision. When we meet him at the beginning of the play he is somewhat worried by the fact that hope keeps sneaking up on him even though he knows how awful everything is. The play uses his life to explain to him that he is the psychological stereotype I discussed above. Then, perversely hopeful in a terrible world full of potential killers like himself, he goes off to meet the girl. Although there are lines to suggest that Quentin is undergoing some kind of torment, the pain of his self-analysis is belied by the discursive, man-to-man stance which he takes during the narrative sections of the play. The remembered scenes, then, do not have the look of experiences being undergone, but of illustrations to prove a point. Even if we were to believe that Quentin is actually coming to conclusions as we watch him, those conclusions—his acceptance of himself—do not lead logically nor dramatically to Holga. It is as though he stepped to the front of the stage and said: "I have a few hours to kill before I meet a plane. Let me spend it describing the human condition."

In *Incident at Vichy* there is the same kind of disconnection between the lesson Von Berg learns and his decision to die for Leduc. Some time ago in *The New York Times* David Ross, reviewing a number of his fellow poets, said of one that she had fallen prey to "the thematic fallacy, the idea that lofty subjects are what make great poetry." [3] Miller seems to be suffering from the same fallacy in *After the Fall* and *Incident at Vichy*.

The disappointment that many of us feel at the new plays should not be taken as a condemnation of Miller's work. He is still one of our most important playwrights, with three good plays and one extremely fine one to his credit. To have written *Death of a Salesman* is an achievement of such significance that Arthur Miller can be allowed a slip, or even a *Fall*.

[3] David Ross, "A Matter of Image," *The New York Times Book Review*, February 21, 1965, p. 4.

PART **III**

The Makers

9 THE PROBLEMS OF THE PRODUCER

Richard Barr

We have often been asked where the new American playwrights are, and, before I go any further and attempt to guess where they are, I perhaps had better tell you who the "we" of us is. It is an organization called Theater 1967, the heads of which are myself, Richard Barr; Edward Albee, the playwright; and my partner, Clinton Wilder. We began in 1960, when we called ourselves Theater 1960, with the off-Broadway presentation of Edward Albee's *The Zoo Story,* his first play to be produced in this country. It was combined with Samuel Beckett's *Krapp's Last Tape* and, fortunately, they proved to be a great hit. But that is not the whole story. It proved to be one of the first times in many, many years that a playwright in this country (probably since O'Neill, as a matter of fact) has had a play produced off-Broadway or in a small theater, risen to fame, and eventually become one of the leading playwrights of the country.

What has actually happened is that since the war there has been a revolution in the method of producing and presenting theater in this country. Long before the war, in the twenties and thirties, it was a relatively cheap proposition to put on a play. Most producers capitalized the plays with their own money. On five to ten thousand dollars, then, you could bring out a very respectable production. When you got into a twenty-five- or thirty-thousand-dollar production, you were really going for the more extravagant ones. After the war, all the costs rose. The situation changed in the theaters themselves. The unions demanded more money for their members, real estate taxes went up, and obviously theater costs went up too. Consequently, instead of costing from five to ten to twenty or even, let us say, thirty thousand dollars to finance a show, it began to take one hundred fifteen, one hundred twenty, or one hundred thirty thousand, and this brought about a system which required individual producers, who did not have that kind of money, to go out and seek funds from backers, as we call them—in other words, the general public. Now, when you do this, you have suddenly become a businessman with a business to care for, and you have moved a bit away from an expression of an art form. What resulted was a great decrease in the number of plays that were produced on Broadway. As I remember, in the early days of Broadway there were often a hundred plays running at a time; now twenty-five or thirty is a remarkable total. And the number of plays produced in a season has dwindled from some five hundred to sixty, seventy, depending on the season. This brought about another change in the theater. Over and above the economics, it created a great division of power. The producer had usually been the boss of his own plays. Now because he had to secure a big-name star in order to raise the needed one hundred fifty thousand dollars capital, the producer would very often sacrifice a certain amount of that power. On occasion he would also seek a name director in order to capitalize the production and sometimes even name designers or costume designers. What this obviously did was to divide the production power, with the bulk of it unfortunately sometimes going to the individual with the strongest personality and ego. The playwright also began to slip into the background. In the first place, there were very few important playwrights in this country; there were certainly some who were quite successful, but not very many important ones who had literary quality. Consequently, it became more and more difficult for playwrights to get their plays produced. Even when they were presented, they were very often torn apart by the various powers just described. This led to a change in the producing system. Obviously plays were going to be written by people interested in theater as an art form,

not just as a business. Thus off-Broadway was born. The definition of off-Broadway is any theater not in the concentrated area
between Forty-first Street and Fifty-second Street, in the Broadway theater district. These range in size from theaters which have
one hundred twenty seats to those which have large seating capac-
ities but which are far from the center of the theater district and
are not used for what we call first-class productions. This does not
mean that the productions are not good; it simply means that
they are not considered first-class Broadway productions. The
most important off-Broadway theater began in 1952 when Brooks
Atkinson, who was and had been for many years the leading critic
on *The New York Times,* went to see a revival of Tennessee Williams' *Summer and Smoke,* which had not been successful in its
1948 Broadway presentation. It opened in a former Sheridan
Square night club by a group calling itself Circle in the Square,
the name they also gave their theater because it presented theater-
in-the-round (actually, three-quarters-round) and because it was
located near Sheridan Square. The play brought fame to Geral-
dine Page, a superb actress, and to José Quintero, who is still a
leading director of American theater. The reputation the group
gained by the one production led to the recognition of off-Broadway by the first-string critics. Before that time, very few productions outside the Times Square area were given any notice in the
newspapers. After Atkinson's reviews appeared, the other critics
began to attend performances, and theaters began to blossom all
over the Greenwich Village area and the downtown Second Ave-
nue district. A great many exciting productions occurred during
the ten- or fifteen-year period after the origination of *Summer
and Smoke* and Circle in the Square in 1952. Several new playwrights came to the front. A new theater group was formed,
called the Living Theater; they are now playing in certain European countries. They began to produce very experimental plays
by new playwrights; the Circle in the Square, however, stuck to
revivals and had very few new playwrights. The Living Theater
presented a play by Jack Gelber called *The Connection,* which
caused quite a bit of fuss. The daily critics more or less dismissed

it, but the magazine critics, who very often take more time with their reviews and in some cases have better literary backgrounds, reviewed it very favorably, and I personally think it was a very important play. The group grew as a result of that success, presenting a variety of plays of Gelber, William Carlos Williams, and others. About the time that the Living Theater began the Gelber production, I decided to go off-Broadway. Actually I had produced on Broadway under the adverse conditions that I described earlier; I had become discouraged with the theater because I wanted to treat it as an art form not a business venture. Neither I nor my partners are very much interested in the sheer business of the commercial theater; we are far more concerned with raising the level of the American theater to that of the other creative arts, such as painting, music, and architecture. American theater is traditionally about twenty-five to forty years behind European theater. I think it has taken a leap to a great extent because of off-Broadway, and off-off-Broadway, which I will discuss later. *The Zoo Story,* which we took to off-Broadway, had been given to me by a friend in an agency. It had been turned down by most producers because they did not know what to do with the one-act play. Despite the fact that *The Zoo Story* is now considered classic and conventional, it was at that time considered avant-garde; Samuel Beckett's *Krapp's Last Tape,* which we also presented, was then considered incomprehensible. It is, of course, now taught in high schools and colleges, and people do not find Beckett as evasive as they did less than a decade ago. To us, the remarkable thing is that most of this has occurred in the last several years. *The Zoo Story* was a great success, and the name Edward Albee became known in the press. We pushed this because we strongly felt that the Broadway system was extremely unfair to the playwright. Consequently, we gathered around us people who would respect the playwright's intention to develop the play as he intended it rather than superimpose their personalities as actors or directors on the playwright. We were very fortunate in having with us at the time Alan Schneider, the director. Alan was a very close friend of Beckett's, and it is really through him that we got permission to do *Krapp's Last Tape.* We had known of Alan's work, but we had not met him, nor had we known how faithful a director he was to a playwright's intention, as opposed to the many directors who superimpose their own personality, distort, and actually change texts without the playwright's permission even though he is present. Alan will have none of this and we were impressed with the way he worked. Consequently, when Edward Albee wrote *The American Dream,* we asked Alan to direct it. He has since then directed all of Albee's plays in this country. The other memebers of our group off-Broadway at that time understood our intention. We did not use star names and therefore we did not have the problem with actors that Broadway had. We had also found a young designer, William Ritman, who since has designed all but one of Albee's plays, and he completed our team. With this approach, the playwright of course emerged as the boss. Albee had not had much theater experience; in fact, he had had practically none when he wrote *The Zoo Story.* Therefore the producers, myself, and Clinton Wilder, on occasion acted as interpreters for Albee until he gained experience. Of course Albee is now as well versed in stagecraft, if not better versed, than any of us, although we have been involved in theater longer than he has; we will still interpret for him whenever it becomes necessary, but he was and remains the key figure in any production we do.

Our production of *The American Dream* became a success. Presented on a double program with *The Death of Bessie Smith,* it enjoyed a long run. It was at this time that Albee began to write *Who's Afraid of Virginia Woolf?* When we first read this drama about a year before our production in 1963, we all felt (Schneider, Wilder, my associates, and myself) that this was an extraordinary piece of work, certainly one of the most important plays written by an American in a very long time. And we were concerned, seriously concerned, about its reception on Broadway by the major newspaper critics. Unfortunately we in the American theater are very dependent upon the critical reception that we receive in the daily papers, particularly in *The New York Times.*

If the critics find favor with a play, it usually meets with success; if they do not like it, rarely can it rise above the critical disfavor. Thus we worried that *Who's Afraid of Virginia Woolf?* might turn out to be a five-day failure, that is, it might open on Tuesday and close on Saturday. And we did not want to expose Albee to this, so we felt that it might be clever to open this new play both on and off-Broadway on the same night. This, we thought, would get wide critical reaction. We felt also that regardless of the critics' reception, we could run a play of this stature off-Broadway indefinitely and thereby keep Albee's name alive before the public rather than risk a premature death, like that met by many another playwright who has gone to Broadway perhaps a bit too early. I am glad we did not carry out this plan; the reason we did not was because on the surface it looked like a stunt, and it was not intended as one. It was meant to be a serious approach to a problem facing the American theater. Therefore, we found the best actors we could, and Alan Schneider and Bill Ritman prepared it for Broadway. The rest is history, of course. Albee's original script was very little changed; perhaps a total of five pages were cut out. None of the four actors involved requested script changes, which, let me tell you, is most unusual on Broadway; needless to say, Alan Schneider followed the text perfectly and the play was presented exactly as Albee intended it. Unfortunately this is fairly rare in American theater, although it should be standard.

What has happened to the playwrights who have not had the fortune to grow out of this type of off-Broadway group is rather interesting. There is a new movement in existence. For instance, Jack Richardson had two plays presented. Two of William Hanley's plays have been presented, *Slow Dance on the Killing Ground* and *Mrs. Dally Has a Lover,* which we first presented at the Cherry Lane Theater; it was first done off-Broadway, then on. Playwrights Terrence McNally, David Raephel, and Oliver Hailey have had rather resounding failures on Broadway; I believe the reason for this is that the plays they presented were not ready for Broadway production. Nevertheless, there have been five or six new playwrights, among them Murray Schisgal, whose play *Luv* has been a great success. Even so, not enough playwrights came from off-Broadway, and this brought about another change. Off-Broadway began to imitate Broadway. Productions that used to cost between five and seven thousand dollars began to cost seventeen, twenty-seven, and, in the case of Kopit's *Oh, Dad, Poor Dad,* over fifty thousand dollars. One cannot survive off-Broadway under those circumstances, and unfortunately there were not enough permanent groups who really knew the problems and economics of theater, and many amateurs entered the field. As a result, there has been quite a lull off-Broadway during the last few years. The number of productions has substantially diminished and so has their quality. The number of new playwrights presented also has gone way down; in fact, ours is the only group that concentrates solely on the presentation of new playwrights (at our Cherry Lane Theatre). We do not do revivals except of our own works; we have actually revived *The American Dream* and *The Zoo Story* some five and seven times each. This is the first time in America that plays have been revived that often by the organization which originally created them.

When the playwrights found the off-Broadway situation becoming untenable, they went to what we now call off-off-Broadway. Off-off-Broadway is really the coffeehouses and, believe it or not, the churches; there are four key areas where it occurs. Off-off-Broadway is any place, not actually a theater where performances are given, and in almost all cases there is no charge made. People come and drink coffee and pay for that but the show is free, or they go to the church and may make a donation but the performance is free and the actors and the director are not paid. This is where the young people—the twenty-year-olds, the twenty-five-year-olds, and some a little older—are writing and working. Most of what they are doing is pretty dreadful, but the important thing is that there is a place where they do get their plays presented. Playwrights who formerly might have despaired and quit writing because they did not have the necessary fifteen or one hundred fifty thousand dollars to produce their plays now are writing scripts. This is because today it is possible to have a piece presented at a place like the Caffé Cino. Joe Cino has done about one play a week for three years, which is a fairly remarkable record. The other coffeehouse that is very prominent is called the Café La Mama, run by Ellen Stewart. Seating approximately eighty or ninety people, Café La Mama had to be made into a club to get around New York zoning laws. Ellen charges a dollar for the coffee and the rest is free; if you want to make a contribution, you can. In the past couple of years, she has presented a number of plays, and out of her group have come playwrights who are now receiving Rockefeller grants. I think another playwright was awarded a Guggenheim grant, which means the young people are finding a market and an ear for their work and are able to present it in these rather confined, almost amateurish conditions. But in producing their plays they gain experience, and in my opinion that is the value of these places.

The other two off-off-Broadway spots are the Judson Memorial Church and St. Mark's in the Bouwerie, both of which have very enlightened religious leaders who insist upon using the church as part of the community. No censorship is exercised. As a matter of fact, some of the pieces presented are extremely questionable, shall we say, with respect to language and taste, but the ministers do not interfere; they let the young playwrights and actors express themselves freely. These off-off-Broadway places are where, I think, the young playwrights can be found today. I am not certain that our next important or exciting new playwrights are going to be a result of the coffeehouses or churches, but I think it is very likely that this is where they will have received their first theater experience. Their first successful play will not be produced in coffeehouses or churches, but they will have gained from these places the experience needed to write more important works. If this occurs, and I believe it will, we will have in this country within the next decade as remarkable, as exciting a group of new talented playwrights as exists anywhere in the world. If it does not, I am afraid that it will take a long time before we again have the opportunity. I would like to add one point that has little to do with where the new playwrights are but rather with what the new playwrights are writing. During the last six or more years, my colleagues and I have between us read over two thousand plays—by that I mean two thousand new plays by new playwrights from all parts of the country and from some foreign countries. These plays come to us at the Cherry Lane and at our office, and it has been our policy to read them all. As a result of reading this many plays, we have chosen about twenty-five of the best writers. Some of these writers are in the coffeehouses I mentioned before, some have been presented off-Broadway, but most of them are brand-new writers who have never been seen. We have formed what we call Theater 67's Playwrights Unit, and we produce their plays, charging no admission to the public, much the same as the coffeehouses do. However, we play in our own theater, the Cherry Lane, or another one which we may rent for the occasion. These plays are done by the best professional actors and directors we can find who are available and willing to give their time; they have been very generous, I might add, to come to the theater, rehearse for a couple of weeks, and present these plays two or three times. The content of the plays themselves is most interesting. We have often been accused of being a theater-of-the-absurd because we have shown the plays of Beckett and Ionesco and Genet and Arabal and several others; Albee himself has been listed among the playwrights-of-the-absurd. Actually, we feel very strongly about this. In the first place, the term "theater-of-the-absurd" was coined by Martin Esslin, and Esslin himself suggests that he was just talking about a collection of playwrights, not a particular school of playwrights; furthermore, he does not include Albee in this group at all. In my opinion, there is a big difference between those who are called the playwrights-of-the-absurd and the younger men who are now writing. Genet, Beckett, Ionesco, and possibly Harold Pinter, are, though they are all alive, really playwrights of the pre-World War II generation. They are writing about themes and subjects that do not pertain to us as much as they did to their own generation. They are writing about the human condition, and of course we are concerned with the human condition in this country, but our playwrights are moving much further along in my opinion; they are far more concerned with the self-awareness of the individual. They are continually examining themselves or others or the characters in their plays with the existential attitude that the individual must take action on his own behalf in order to be able to live in the present-day world. And these dramatists are writing plays in a newly realistic vein, not in the abstract vein of *Waiting for Godot, Happy Days,* or Beckett's drama called *Play,* nor with the strange settings of some of Ionesco's plays. Actually they take place in living rooms and homes, in bars or stations, in actual spots that we can recognize. *Who's Afraid of Virginia Woolf?* is a prime example: it is set in the living room of a college professor in New England. The themes of these current plays are heightened to a point that does not necessarily reflect the nature of their setting. Sometimes the themes vary and are so extraordinary that no setting is necessary at all; however, this would not be generally true of the plays of Genet, Ionesco, and Beckett. This is a whole new field, one which I think can probably be expressed in three words—Myth, Illusion, and Satire. This is where I think American playwrights are headed.

10 AN INTERVIEW WITH EDWARD ALBEE

Q.: *Mr. Albee, would you tell us something about your background and why you chose to go into the theater rather than some other means of expression?*

ALBEE: First, let me say that it is very nice, if not too common, to find the playwright involved in a discussion of the American theater. One of the great problems with the American theater from a playwright's point of view is that it seems to consist of buildings and actors and producers and an audience but very seldom of playwrights. What prompted me to become involved in the theater rather than something sensible, I suppose, is what you really mean. Well, we have to go back a few years to when I was six years old, when I decided to be a writer and started writing poetry. There was a brief period of half a year when I was eleven when I gave up writing and decided to be a composer. That only lasted for a half year. So I decided when I was six to be a writer, I suppose on the assumption it was going to be simpler and easier than working. I found out differently, of course. By the time I was twenty-six, my poetry in the twenty-year period had gotten somewhat better than it was when I was six. Not much, but some—not enough, though, to allow me to call myself a poet. When I was fifteen I wrote my first novel. When I was seventeen, I wrote my second novel. With the possible exception of some novel I don't know about somewhere, they are probably the two worst novels ever written by an American. And being what I laughingly call a creative writer, I don't think very clearly and therefore I couldn't write essays. So by the time I was hitting my late twenties, which in this youth-conscious culture of ours is the end of the world, I was still determined to be a writer and there really wasn't much left to do but to start writing plays. Perhaps the fact that my family was peripherally involved with the theater and started sending me to plays when I was five years old had something to do with it. Perhaps the fact that I started reading plays—something that most people never do, unfortunately—when I was about ten or eleven had something to do with it. Whether it was simply because there was nothing else I felt I could try or whether some other things were involved, I don't know.

Q.: *Isn't it true that you say you were a failure as a novelist but that you had your first play produced?*

ALBEE: Indeed, my first play wasn't a novel. I am not trying to suggest that in the long run I won't turn out to be a failure as a playwright either, but when I started writing plays as a sort of thirtieth-birthday present to myself, for the first time in the twenty-four years I had been a writer I had the curious feeling, not of accomplishment exactly, but that I was doing something I felt comfortable with. The fact that it seems to have worked out in the past six or seven years that what I feel comfortable doing seems to make enough people uncomfortable to give me a certain amount of success is something I don't know about. Indeed, my first play, *The Zoo Story*, was produced within about a year after I wrote it; it was presented in West Berlin in German and then six months after that it was produced in the United States. Since that time I have written seven, eight, or nine plays, I can never remember how many, and they have all been produced, too, with relative degrees of commercial or critical success or failure.

Q.: *Do you think it surprising that your first production should have been done in Germany rather than in the United States?*

ALBEE: I suppose I should be surprised about it, but when I wrote my first play I had no idea what one did or what happened to a play when one had written it. I was so totally innocent as to what occurred as a professional in the theater that, no, I wasn't surprised to find myself in West Berlin watching *The Zoo Story* in German. It was a very nice experience and the first and only time, of course, that I would ever be able to see the very first production of my first play. Ever since then, to a certain extent my plays have struck me as making more sense in languages I don't understand than in English.

Q.: *They all have been presented in various European theaters, haven't they?*

ALBEE: Yes, I have seen plays of mine done in Germany, France, Czechoslovakia, and in England which, of course, is a different——

Q.: *A different language?*

ALBEE: Quite a different language, yes. I have missed quite a number of productions of my plays I have wanted to see. I haven't seen any Japanese productions, for example, or any of the Latin American productions.

Q.: *Of course, we get a return on this, that is to say plays from foreign theaters come to America more easily than they used to, don't you think?*

ALBEE: Well, when you consider the commercial theater, by which I mean Broadway in this country, there is a kind of inverse chauvinism and the plays accepted most readily and returned to, with the exception of a few sex comedies, are usually imported plays. As a matter of fact, the majority of the producers in the commercial theater aren't producers, they are merely import-export people. But this is limited pretty much, at least the success of them, to English and French plays, and most of the French plays are butchered by their translators, or adapters, rather.

Q.: *Do you think this is for economic reasons?*

ALBEE: The butchering?

Q.: *No, the importation. That is to say, you have a success, therefore perhaps you can be sure it will succeed here.*

ALBEE: I am not quite certain what the reason is. Naturally, the importation of a play by Harold Pinter is usually a good idea, and if we can get a play by Anouilh brought over intact, that would be a good idea, too, but this very seldom happens. After all, there are a lot of good plays being written in Europe these days, but the mass-importation of European musicals and comedies that are certainly no worse or no better than our own strikes me as being sloth.

Q.: *This butchery in the translations or adaptations, is it willful or is it an attempt to adjust to what they think an American audience would take?*

ALBEE: I don't know which is less comforting to consider—that it is conscious butchering to produce a product for a pre-sold market or that it is unconscious butchery due to poor aesthetics. They are both rather unhappy situations. There does seem to be the assumption that a play by Anouilh, for example, can't be understood or accepted on its own terms and own level. The last one that did come over, of course, was *Poor Bitos,* which was a very good play and wasn't adapted to American taste, so the critics slapped it down very quickly. There is no need for it. I think it is primarily a kind of commercialism, that is all.

Q.: *Do you feel that Broadway itself is responsible for the low condition of the American theater? Let me put that another way, do you think that until the theater manages to work away from Broadway, from New York City, it will be in this shackled condition?*

ALBEE: I am not one of those people who feel that spreading the theater out around the country is necessarily going to solve all its problems. After all, what you would be doing is merely moving the bad taste out of New York and infecting the rest of the country. It seems to me that until the vicious round robin of misunderstanding between critic and audience vanishes you are going to have very bad theater. The majority of influential critics, theater critics, feel, and I may quote Walter Kerr—or paraphrase him rather—who remarked that the majority of the important critics feel it is their responsibility to reflect what they understand to be the taste of their readers. This was one of the most staggering remarks Mr. Kerr ever made in public. The audience, on the other hand, assumes that its taste is fashioned by the critic, by the same critic who believes that his function is to represent the audience's taste. The audience in the main has come to the conclusion that theater is a buyer's market, that the theater should be full of entertainments fashioned to the taste of the audience; it has become a rather lazy audience. Until the audience is willing to go to the theater as an adventure, a participation rather than an escape, and until the critic stops pandering to the extension of this public demand for status quo, we are going to have very bad theater and I don't think moving the whole system outside New York is going to help any.

Q.: *But might you not find a fresh audience outside New York?*

ALBEE: Yes, you might, but a fresh audience can be corrupted very easily by the same nonsense the New York audience receives and seems to want.

Q.: *Do you see any possible help from, let's say, the colleges or the universities, which now try to train people for the theater and also try, I think, to train audiences for the theater?*

ALBEE: Well, when I went to college a long, long time ago, the year and a half that college and I could stand each other, the theater portion of modern-literature courses stopped with early Bernard Shaw. Nowadays I understand that people like Sam Beckett and Jean Genet are taught in the theater section, which is very important. I don't really know what value university has in training actors. I don't think that playwrights can ever be trained. I am sure there are examples to prove me wrong here, but the enormous value that the university can have, it seems to me, is to corrupt the future theater audience, to corrupt it into expecting and demanding more of the theater than they now get. That could be of enormous value. After all, most of the kids who are in college now will go to sleep mentally within five years after they graduate out anyway, but it would be nice to think there is a whole generation of college people that expected more interesting things in the theater: they might then possibly get some good theater. It is very difficult to change the people who are already set in their ways, but this positive corruption can take place on the college level nicely.

> Q.: *It seems to me that the most enthusiastic audience for playwrights like Genet and Beckett and yourself indeed are college-student audiences. Do you agree?*

ALBEE: I have noticed that on off-Broadway—which is, of course, the much more interesting of the two theaters in New York, and which does better, more adventurous plays—the audiences do tend to be quite young and enthusiastic. It would be nice if we could get this into the commercial theater, too.

> Q.: *Is there any relationship or analogy between what happened in the American theater after World War I, when there was a strong creative and imaginative impulse in what was then off-Broadway—the O'Neill Theatre down in the Village, etc.—and what has been going on in the last five or ten years?*

ALBEE: Certainly, there is a relationship. Why this always happens after wars, I don't know. It is a shame we have to have the wars to produce the results. It is true that in the past ten years, mainly as a result of the playwrights who emerged in France directly after World War II, there has been a great deal more excitement about theater among those who really care about it. And the whole temperament, environment, has changed so much. I think every other person walking around Greenwich Village in New York is a playwright these days. Most are pretty bad, but at least the models they work from are much more interesting.

> Q.: *I know you have been working with some of these young playwrights. Would you explain this adventurous theater that you and Mr. Barr and Mr. Wilder are engaged in?*

ALBEE: Sure, it is really a very simple operation. It occurred to us that since criticism is in such a bad state in this country—that is, most of our critics aren't interested in adventurous theater and certainly don't like off-Broadway—it was dangerous to expose exciting new playwrights immediately to the "six dead men." So what we have done is to set up a workshop [the Playwrights

Unit] in an off-Broadway theater, a two-hundred-seat theater. We have about thirty-five young playwrights—the number fluctuates between thirty and forty—who are free to use our theater. We provide them with actors and directors and an audience, if they want one, and they can experiment with their plays and see them presented in front of an invited audience without having to face the critic too early. They seem to get something out of it.

Q.: *Why do you say "an audience, if they want one"? I can't imagine a playwright not wanting an audience.*

ALBEE: Well, if a playwright comes in with a work in progress and is merely interested in seeing whether he is going in the right direction, whether it works on stage for him, then he doesn't have to have an audience. In other words, it is a laboratory for the playwright to work in free from commercial pressure.

Q.: *Where do these young men come from? From what sort of background?*

ALBEE: I think every other person I see in Greenwich Village is a playwright; they all have play scripts under their arms. They may have always been around, but perhaps the environment of the past five or ten years has been such that they have suddenly emerged; perhaps the good soil produced them automatically.

Q.: *Are there some models that appeal to them?*

ALBEE: I would say, offhand, that people like Beckett and Ionesco and Genet and Pinter and a few others have suggested to young people, ones who used to write novels all the time, that the theater can be an interesting and exciting place.

Q.: *Haven't you said some rather sharp things about the critics, Mr. Albee?*

ALBEE: I have only said sharp things about the critics because in the main they have been nice to me and I can afford to be accurate. Without it sounding like sour grapes.

Q.: *You say they don't like off-Broadway. Well, Mr. Atkinson is not currently a critic, but certainly he gave full support to off-Broadway. Don't you agree?*

ALBEE: Indeed, seven or eight years ago starting with Mr. Atkinson's good work and followed by Mr. Watts of the *Post,* the critics started to pay attention to off-Broadway and off-Broadway burgeoned from ten productions a year up to two hundred forty at one point a few years ago. Then reaction started setting in. I think the critics, or rather the majority of them, but not all because there are still some pretty good men, seem to feel that the avant-garde has been given quite enough attention, and also, as I said before, it was becoming too much work for them. The result is that the first-string critics for the most part don't go off-Broadway anymore, and the audience, the readers of these reviews, have been conditioned to believe only what the first-string critics say, never the second-string critics, so there has been a reaction against the experimental theater in New York.

Q.: *Do you really feel that the critics have this much power on audience response?*

ALBEE: They have this much power because, for the most part, the audience refuses to think for itself. For example, let me bring myself into it, though I don't usually like to. One of the last plays I had produced was a little comedy called *Tiny Alice*. We had two weeks of previews in the New York theater before the critics came to see the play. The audiences were quite vocal in their response. Some people booed and hissed, others said "bravo." There were arguments, loud arguments, in the audience during the previews. Also, from the comments I could hear, the majority of the people certainly had opinions about the play. Then the critics saw it and informed the public that the play was really too complicated, too difficult or too confused (as opposed to confusing) to understand. From that point on, the audiences that went to see *Tiny Alice* went into the theater confused. Now, these were exactly the same type of people who, before the critics told them they couldn't understand the play, were understanding it fine. This leads me to the conclusion that the audience doesn't think for itself quite enough.

Q.: *Then, you not only want them to think for themselves but to react to the play, isn't that so, Mr. Albee?*

ALBEE: Indeed.

Q.: *I think a good many playwrights are content if the au-*

*dience becomes involved and perhaps forgets about itself for
an hour or two. What are your feelings?*

ALBEE: I don't think that's enough. Mind you, I am not trying to
suggest that there be a total revolution and the good kind of
theater take over completely. I think it is fine if the musicals go
right on, and the comedies, the plays manufactured for the present audience's taste, but there must be a certain coexistence. I
think the theater is also an arena of engagement, of argument, of
participation, of putting the audience more into itself rather than
taking it out of itself. If we look at the majority of plays that have
survived for any length of time in Western culture, they haven't
been the plays that have taken the audience out of itself but those
that have put the audience into itself.

Q.: *What about the movement, which I think is probably
dead now or dying, instituted by Brecht, where you "alienate" the audience, you lecture to the audience, you don't
allow the audience really to become involved?*

ALBEE: One of the most interesting things about Brecht as a
playwright, and the reason that he is a good playwright when he
is, is that in his very best plays the work of art transcends the
theory. Take such excellent Brecht plays as *Mother Courage* and
Resistible Rise of Artur Ui and a couple of others, indeed, I suppose you are having the lecture, you are having the propaganda,
but the plays transcend their didactic nature and become involving experiences. You can teach at the same time as you are engaging. I think perhaps that the entire theory of alienation is a little
misunderstood by the majority of the people who use the term. Of
course, it is not an attempt to alienate the audience but merely
an attempt to keep the audience at a sufficient distance so that
two things are happening simultaneously, that the audience is
being objective about an experience that it is having. It is really
not very different from the way an audience should ideally be
approached in any play.

Q.: *It is substitute for allegory, perhaps?*

ALBEE: Yes, perhaps.

Q.: *It always struck me as rather medieval, as a matter of fact. Are you aware of an allegorical tendency in your own writing?*

ALBEE: I try not to be aware of anything in my own writing. I think it is very dangerous for a writer to start thinking about himself in the third person, to start examining what he has been writing and what he is writing for its implications, its content and its relationship to what he has done before, its relationship to what other people have done before. There is sufficiently little spontaneity in the theater, and unless you are a pure didactic playwright like Shaw or Brecht, then I think it is best if you don't think about it too much.

Q.: *However, you do spend a long time thinking about your plays before you write them?*

ALBEE: Yes, but when I get to the point where I have thought about them sufficiently, then I try to turn my thoughts off and let the unconscious work as much as possible.

Q.: *How do you know when you have reached that point?*

ALBEE: When the characters I have been thinking about have become more real than the people around me and they start informing me that it is time to write them down, then I go to the typewriter.

Q.: Tiny Alice, *for example?*

ALBEE: I don't know how long I thought about it. When I say I think about the plays before I write them down, I don't mean I sit in a chair for eight hours and think. I can't think for more than a couple of hours at a time or I get a very bad headache. However, I suppose I had been thinking about that play for a year and a half because I do recall, or somebody pointed out to me rather, that I mentioned I was going to write that play fully two years before I did write it, so obviously I must have been thinking about it. But the nature of the thinking is, well, it's rather strange; it's merely a writer's method of thinking, which is involving himself in bits and pieces of the situation and testing the characters' validity in situations that won't occur in the play, for example, until the reality is reached.

Q.: *In other words, are you generally thinking about two or three plays at the same time?*

ALBEE: Yes, I usually am.

Q.: *Do you have an internal repertory?*

ALBEE: If a play were thought out completely before one went to the typewriter, I don't imagine anybody would ever write one down because there would be no interest and no surprise; it would merely be an exercise in typing.

Q.: *But this, I think, is probably the method that is taught in play-writing courses, isn't it?*

ALBEE: Well, most playwrights in play-writing courses, if they're taught by a playwright, are urged unconsciously, perhaps, to write like that playwright, but if they're not taught by the playwright, the urging is to write like other models. I have not seen many play-writing courses where a playwright was urged to write like himself.

Q.: *What playwrights do you feel have had a particular influence on you?*

ALBEE: Well I suppose——

Q.: *At the beginning?*

ALBEE: In one way or another, every single playwright one has ever experienced is an influence, because influence is a matter of selection, acceptance, and rejection. Therefore I imagine I have been influenced by all sorts of playwrights whose work I don't like as well as by ones I do like. Specifically, however, I do think that my exposure to Beckett and to late O'Neill was probably important right at the time I gave up poetry and the novel.

Q.: *By late O'Neill, do you mean* Long Day's Journey into Night?

ALBEE: Yes, and *The Iceman Cometh* and those of that period when he started writing good plays.

Q.: *Do you mean after he got over his gimmicky period?*

ALBEE: Yes.

Q.: *What about Thornton Wilder? The European theater is full of Wilder.*

ALBEE: The only thing I feel about Mr. Wilder is I wish he would write more plays. He has a wonderful play, the *Alcestiade,* which had been done in Europe—in Edinburgh and Germany— and which he won't allow to be done in this country. I don't know why. I think he is an extraordinarily good playwright and I'm usually incensed when people list important playwrights and they all seem to forget to include Mr. Wilder. He is one of our most interesting playwrights.

Q.: *I think this is because he doesn't produce regularly; it is easy to forget in the theater. All your plays, I think, have been done in various European and, I guess, Asian theaters. Isn't this true?*

ALBEE: I mentioned Japan earlier, but I don't know about the rest of Asia. Certainly all over Europe.

Q.: *Have you seen many of the European productions?*

ALBEE: As I said before, I have seen productions in France and Germany and Czechoslovakia and Italy. I know there have been productions elsewhere.

Q.: *As you see these productions, do you notice any important differences between European method of production and performance and American?*

ALBEE: Occasionally there will be some misunderstanding. For example, two of my short plays, *The Zoo Story* and *The American Dream,* were done in Paris recently. *The Zoo Story* was done superbly, with complete understanding. *The American Dream* was as bad as any high-school production of a play of mine I have ever seen. The gratifying thing I have discovered about my own work is that it doesn't seem particularly exotic to European audiences. That is nice. There are minor differences, I suppose the tempo and the nature of audience response, but I've never felt that an audience was misunderstanding a play except in that one production of *The American Dream* in Paris.

Q.: *Have you ever been moved to write a film script?*

ALBEE: No, I haven't. I have been thinking about it, of course. But I feel at this point that I don't think visually enough yet, and if I ever did write a film script I would want to direct it myself.

Q.: *I notice you were not involved in the filming of* Virginia Woolf. *Why?*

ALBEE: I tried for a year and a half to become involved in it and to have the film made on my own terms, but that didn't work out so I let greed take over.

Q.: *How can you bear to see your child being reshaped by other hands?*

ALBEE: By convincing myself that the movies are an unreal form.

Q.: *Unreal?*

ALBEE: Unreal and don't exist and therefore I don't feel protective about them. It is very hard to take American movies seriously.

Q.: *It has been said, of course, that the movies have replaced the theater of naturalism. Is this true?*

ALBEE: I don't think the movies have replaced anything, in this country certainly. I don't feel that anybody in the United States goes to an American movie and believes it and takes it seriously for one moment, anymore than they do television.

Q.: *What about the critics?*

ALBEE: Well, they are paid to take it seriously.

11 AN INTERVIEW WITH MURRAY SCHISGAL

Q.: *Mr. Schisgal, the lives of Americans are so diverse, their resources are so different, their backgrounds are so unalike that I think, to begin with, it would be interesting if we knew something about your experience. By what route did you come to playwriting?*

SCHISGAL: I am afraid by a rather irregular route. Originally I started our writing novels and short stories, but I was unable to get any of them published. I wrote four novels and nearly sixty-five short stories over a period of ten to fifteen years and after a while, out of frustration, I turned to writing plays, and I seem to have been a bit more lucky with them.

Q.: *But what did you do before you started writing?*

SCHISGAL: Well, I always managed to have one job or another while I was writing. I have worked as a teacher in the New York City school system. I practiced law for a couple of years. For a time, when I got out of the service, I was a musician. It was always necessary to do something to support myself, but while working I always managed to find a few hours each day to write and I kept that up as well.

Q.: *You have said you began your professional career playing jazz. What instrument?*

SCHISGAL: I played the tenor saxophone, the clarinet, and the flute. When I went to high school we were required to learn to play some kind of musical instrument, and I studied clarinet and became quite interested in it. I took private lessons and played all through high school. Then when I went into the Navy I tried to get into the band, but they wouldn't have it, so I put it aside until I got out of the service. Then I joined up with a couple of other fellows in the neighborhood and we used to play at weddings and at social functions Friday and Saturday nights. It was rather a good life. But after a while I tired of it and, if I remember correctly, I pawned my three instruments for about one hundred fifty dollars and went down to Florida to see a bit of the country.

Q.: *Your current play, Mr. Schisgal, is a great success in New York and has been played in Europe. I wonder if you could say something about how that play came to be? What was the origin of* Luv?

SCHISGAL: The title or the play?

Q.: *Well, both, as a matter of fact.*

SCHISGAL: Well, the play is primarily a satire on the rather ill usage we put the emotion of love to, it is l-o-v-e. It attempts to show just how ridiculously we go about pretending to experience the emotion of love. That generally describes the play, although I hope there is a great deal more to it than that.

Q.: *I know, and I assume most of the readers know, it has been often said that plays are not written but rewritten. I assume that this is true of a play like* Luv, *but, I wonder, do you do your rewriting before the play gets into rehearsal? Or do you do much rewriting as a result of the rehearsal experience?*

SCHISGAL: No, you see, oddly enough the rewriting during rehearsals presents a great danger because there is always the question, How much should a play be altered to suit the specific needs of a specific production? If one is hampered with a bad actor, should one contort and distort one's play so that the bad actor should be able to carry his part of the play? This rewriting during rehearsal is something one can't do too easily because many factors enter into it. I think rewriting should be done primarily before rehearsal, and during rehearsal hopefully only the barest minimum should be changed; the actors and director should be compelled to make come to life the words on the printed page. I think too many plays get ruined at the rehearsal stage by hasty rewriting, rewriting to suit a specific but perhaps very artificial need. Therefore I think that all or most rewriting should come before going into rehearsal, if at all possible of course.

Q.: *I have heard frequently from other playwrights and from reading the papers that audiences sometimes bring about rewriting, that is to say, a producer will have certain particular audiences in mind that he thinks have to be satisfied. Has this been your experience at all?*

SCHISGAL: Well, I do believe in the value of previews—that is, in doing the plays before an audience—and I do believe in the value of listening to the audience and not ignoring them, because they do have something to say to every playwright. But, here again, one must be very careful, because there are all kinds of audiences, and audiences change. I think the danger, of course, is to rely solely on the audience, that is, if they are not laughing, to put in a few jokes; if they are not attentive, to create some excitement on the stage merely to gain their attention. It is something that has to be carefully gauged. What has too frequently happened, of course, and what still happens, is that the audience's response is taken for granted; it becomes the ultimate arbiter of what the play will be. I think this is dangerous because there is no one, two, three, or four audiences that can possibly speak for all audiences. If we travel around the country with a play, we know how different audiences can be; ultimately we must rely upon our own judgment, our own taste, our own perception of what the play should be. If we do that we may go wrong, but at least we won't go crazy.

Q.: *Another factor that I think should affect the production of a play is that, given the economic conditions in the American theater, plays have to run a long time—many months— in order to break even. I don't know about a play with three characters, but many plays certainly don't make money for a long time. Surely this must degenerate it, no?*

SCHISGAL: It probably does, but I must say something here because you did use the phrases "The American theater" and "the economic conditions in the American theater." I have spent much time going to the theater in Europe. I must say I don't see that the economics in the American theater is very different from that of the theater in London, Paris, or elsewhere. I really feel we are reaching a kind of uniformity. To do a play in London in the West End is not cheap. It may not be as expensive as it is here, but nevertheless it costs a substantial amount and all things seem to equate themselves. Therefore this problem of economics in the theater is not specifically or peculiarly American or one confined to the American theater. It is a problem that confronts every major theater in every major city. How it will be solved, I don't know, but to recognize that it is not unique to America is, I think, to recognize the sameness of a problem that exists everywhere in theater.

Q.: *Of course, it is not just true of* on-*Broadway, is it?*

SCHISGAL: No, that's right. The actual root of it, the real rock-bottom question that it raises, has to do with the theater's value in society today. It is no longer merely a question of how much does it cost to produce a play on-Broadway, off-Broadway, or elsewhere. It concerns the validity of the dramatic experience in our own day and age, which we can discuss at length later. But the problem of economics is one that confronts theaters in every major city and I don't think there is an easy solution to it. I really think it is something we have to live with for the moment.

Q.: *What I had in mind before, of course, are the European theaters supported by the government, the Continental theaters, mainly repertory theater.*

SCHISGAL: You know, I recently spent some time in West Berlin. *Luv* is being done there by a repertory theater. It is being shown in the Schlosspark Theatre and is presented three or four times a week in repertory with other plays. From my talks with the German actors, I didn't get the feeling they were very happy with the repertory setup; they felt overworked and underpaid. I didn't get the feeling that because it was repertory theater there weren't economic headaches and other kinds of problems, and ultimately

I didn't find that the repertory theater itself was that much more inspired, more creative, more vital than the commercial theater in other cities of the world.

>   Q.: *That's interesting because we are experiencing a great revival of repertory theater in this country, not just in New York but many cities in the South and West, as if there were something more stimulating about it to the performers. Do you think that this is true?*

SCHISGAL: No, I don't believe that. I am glad that there is such a thing as repertory theater because it frequently makes theater possible where there would be none, and for that we ought to be grateful, but I don't think it is the answer to the ills of the theater. I don't believe that it is by any means a complete nor entirely happy solution, particularly here in America. I don't even know whether repertory theater is really valid insofar as it will offer the public a kind of theater presentation to which they can respond. I am not so sure that repertory theater in this country doesn't take on the mask of something precious, cultish, and removed from the public because it doesn't have to court the public. None of these things seem clear-cut to me. I think the real task at hand is not so much a concern with what kind of theater we should have as with making theater an exciting event that will involve the audience to such an extent that it makes the whole thing worthwhile. This is always brought about by individuals working at their craft and coming up with the kind of excitement we should ask for and expect in a theater; it will not result from debate on the economics of the theater, the value of repertory theater, etc.

>   Q.: *You said before that we might discuss the validity of the dramatic experience in our society. What are your views on this?*

SCHISGAL: I think it is important to examine this subject because too frequently we go to the theater to see a play that either could have been made into a film much more effectively or should have been left as a novel, where it succeeded. Too often that quality which is unique to the theater is completely absent and instead of being asked to share something which could not take place anywhere but in a theater, we are asked to involve ourselves in some kind of dreary melodramatic TV-type play. I think we could insist upon the proper use of the theater without falling prey to speaking just nonsense. Here is where I think the new excitement comes from. If in talking about playwrights since World War II, we mention someone like Genet, we are paying respect to him for bringing theatrical excitement back into the theater, something that could not take place anywhere else but in a theater, something wholly germane to a theater, to actors confronting an audience, and to that specific dramatic moment. It is this awareness of the proper use of the theater—why we are in the theater, why we are asked to go there, what is it we are seeking, what is the reward of being there—that has given it a tremendous impetus in the last few years.

Q.: *You use the word "involvement," the audience's involvement in the performance. There was a movement, originating in Germany, which insisted that the audience should not become involved in a performance in the way that audiences normally become involved in a play of Ibsen's, etc. I don't think these plays ever had much success in this country. I have a feeling that Americans go to the theater to become involved in the performance, don't you?*

SCHISGAL: Are you talking about epic theater? Brecht?

Q.: *Yes.*

SCHISGAL: Well, let me say this about it. I must confess that for me the times when Brecht succeeds in fulfilling his enormous talent are those occasions when, despite himself, he has created a situation in which the audience is involved. In such plays as *Mother Courage* and *Threepenny Opera,* he could talk himself blue in the face about his didactic methods and how he is going to keep the audience at arm's length, but when he becomes the playwright all that is chucked out, and whether he willed it or not he can tug at the heartstrings and involve an audience to as great a degree as any soap-opera craftsman. Perhaps the term "involve" is too restrictive in that sense. I don't mean involved purely in the emotional sense, I mean involved in the sense of having people sitting on the edge of their seats and being so interested that they don't prefer to be elsewhere. I think if you have achieved that, you have done enough. It is that kind of excitement that one feels in front of a good painting or listening to good music, where one does not want to be anywhere else, and one recognizes why one is participating in the event. Too frequently one doesn't know why one is in the theater or what is supposed to come out of it all; one would just as soon be home in bed.

Q.: *What are you trying to do to an audience?*

SCHISGAL: Just what I have said, I think. I am trying to keep them on the edge of their seats and to have them participate with me in what the actors are doing. I think astonishment and awe belong properly in the theater. If I can manage an iota of either emotion, well, that's what I am striving for anyway.

Q.: *Astonishment is certainly a term that associates itself well with comedy. How does awe?*

SCHISGAL: Well, I really don't think of myself as primarily a comedic writer. I frankly write what at the moment strikes me as being worthwhile writing and I just don't categorize myself for what I am doing.

Q.: *But what about* Luv?

SCHISGAL: *Luv* is a comedy, yes, and I am working on a play now which, if everything goes well, will be done here in the city. It is a play called *Jimmy Shine* and that would not be properly speaking a comedy. Although it has comedic things in it, nonetheless I hope it has other things in it as well.

Q.: *Of course, this again is fairly characteristic of the good plays that have come out of America in the last twenty years; that is, however serious or indeed tragic they may be, there are certainly strong comic elements in them. Isn't this so?*

SCHISGAL: Yes, it won't do to adhere to classic distinctions between comedy and tragedy. I don't know if they were ever valid, but certainly they have little use in our vocabulary today. I think a play primarily should not shy away from any attitude which it needs to fulfill itself, and if one would deal with contemporary society, I think that of necessity one has to laugh as much as cry, or something like that.

> Q.: *Since you don't want to be categorized as a comic playwright or tragic playwright, do you have any feeling about being included in the school of the absurd playwrights?*

SCHISGAL: Once again I am not sure of the validity of these definitions. I really think it is a journalistic device to lump together a group of people under a big heading so that a headline is established. I don't know precisely what it means. I do think a better word, or perhaps a better notion of what a number of playwrights are about, is to link modern playwrights, contemporary playwrights, with the notion of existentialism, and that I would describe—and I think I can clarify it so it doesn't sound too esoteric—as a concern for man in a very unique and extreme confrontation with his environs. I think something that deals with men in this extreme position, confronting—as if it were his last hour—his own being, his own state, etc., describes an attitude that contemporary playwrights share. I think it is more closely aligned with what the existential philosophies are concerned with than with the single notion of absurdity.

> Q.: *I think I would agree with you that "absurd" is a journalist's term, and the gentleman who coined it used it first in a book that included every contemporary writer from Genet to Albee. I don't think you had been produced at the time, so you didn't get included in this. But Mr. Albee once said the absurd theater was the realistic theater of Broadway. This has no relevance at all to contemporary life, does it?*

SCHISGAL: I think the excitement that has been brought to the theater today is twofold. One, it is the reintroduction of theatrical values; it is a refusal to ignore them or pretend that they don't exist; it is trying to make the theater something that it can no longer be, and that is a realistic theater, a naturalistic theater. I think the theater of Ibsen and such others has been absolutely replaced by films. I do think that what I said, the excitement of the contemporary theater is (1) the reintroduction of theatrical values, things that can only happen in the theater, things that take into account an audience, an actor, and their physical confrontation; and (2) other than this reintroduction of the theatrical values, I think there is an emphasis on naked man, upon man shorn of all props of identity, of man who is once again in a kind of wilderness trying to establish himself once more as what he is. I am fumbling because the truth of the matter is I don't enjoy talking about it. I would just give you an inkling of the thought, but really, as I speak these words, I am rather self-conscious of them because it becomes theoretical, it becomes pedantic, and I really feel like I am in a kind of trap which I'd like to extricate myself from.

It is unfair to end on that, but perhaps the excitement of the contemporary theater revolves around these two ideas: one is the reintroduction of theatrical values and the other is the emphasis on existential man.

Q.: *Would you say what is going on right now with the newer playwrights is not unlike what happened when Eugene O'Neill came into the theater in the twenties?*

SCHISGAL: Well, that's it. I think it has some similarities, but I think it has even greater disparities—by that I mean that it was possible for O'Neill to write all sorts of plays ranging from symbolism to realism to fantasy. I don't know whether a playwright today can ignore films, for one. I don't think one should allow oneself to do a play which could be made into a better film. Now, if you are going to do a naturalistic play, a play that demands the starkest naturalism, I don't know why one would want to do it in the theater when the camera is obviously a much better vehicle for portraying and depicting naturalism; so I really feel that the theater has because of this become purer and has to utilize those things which were peculiar to the theater, that is, the imaginative things—not only imaginative things, but things such as magic and ceremony and carnival trickery. Burlesque, masks, dances, singing—all the old props of the theater—are back today because this is where they work so wonderfully, but why one would try to do something which can be done much better as a film, I don't know.

Q.: *Is this why you respect Genet, for example?*

SCHISGAL: Yes, that is why I think he enjoys the respect of so many playwrights and people working in the theater, because they recognize it. They are the first to recognize what he is doing, what he is about, and he answers well the question, Why this and why that? And then you know why because this is the kind of vital exciting theater that theaters are built for.

Q.: *Is there anything you would like to say about the current state of the theater in this country?*

SCHISGAL: Yes, I think we have very major problems. I think that there are a great many obstacles to be overcome before one does get a play put on and there are all sorts of pressures that can be exerted on a playwright, but overall, I think, we still manage each season to present a number of first-rate plays, we still manage to have an immense audience in New York City filling some twenty theaters every night, and we still manage to create a theatrical excitement for which there is no other place to go to but a theater.

Q.: *Do you think New York is still the center of the American theater?*

SCHISGAL: Oh, yes, definitely, no question about it. The only way to really get yourself any kind of attention is to be produced in the New York theater, not only the attention of the rest of the United States but also the rest of the world. When something is done in New York, it gets coverage all over. This is important only so far as it helps pay the bills, and if you have another play you want produced it can be done more easily, but there is no doubt that New York remains the most important theatrical center in this country.

Q.: *You mentioned Genet before. I think it is a little surprising how many of these European writers have succeeded,*

*have found audiences in New York and particularly in col-
lege theaters. Do you think that there is a return for this
from the United States to Europe?*

SCHISGAL: Oh, yes, definitely. I also think that there is really only
one theater. We like to talk about the French theater and the
English theater and American theater, but all these distinctions
really kind of melt away. I think we in America, the American
playwrights, are as aware of what is going on in the French and
the English theater as the people over there. No sooner does a
play get itself produced than we usually have the script printed
here or get a copy to read, and the reverse is true. I was in Paris a
while ago, before I went over to West Berlin, to make arrangements with a French actor named Laurent Terzieff, who is doing
Luv there. Now, Laurent did *The Typists* and *The Tiger* in
Paris, and as soon as I finished *Luv,* the same time as I sent the
script to Eli Wallach and Anne Jackson in New York I sent a
copy to Laurent, and he, I am happy to say, responded that he
would do it in Paris. So all these lines kind of fall to the wayside
and I feel just as much at home in the European theater as I do
here.

Q.: *Where have your plays been produced in Europe?*

SCHISGAL: All over. I have had plays produced in Europe that I
haven't had done here yet. I had a play done in Europe called
Ducks and Lovers in 1961, which hasn't been done here yet. Perhaps we will do it one day. Also a one-act play called *Windows*
was done in Copenhagen and that play hasn't been done here yet.
So the theater is even more exciting because it is an international
one, and not only are we able to get our plays done there but
certainly our theater is much richer for the number of European
plays that we present here.

Q.: *Certainly one new aspect of American theater is that it
is international in character. Are there any other new things
being done in American theater?*

SCHISGAL: I hear that things are changing: regional theater is
spreading all over the country; there is theater on college campuses—every major college has a theater of one sort or another.

That it will ever replace the importance of New York, I doubt very much, but it is encouraging and worthwhile to know that the rest of the country isn't without theater. Every city does have a theater of its own, whether it be a local neighborhood one, a college or touring company, or a small repertory theater. And these theaters are growing at an impressive rate. But again let me add that I don't think this will replace New York's importance as a theater city.

12 AN INTERVIEW WITH SHELDON HARNICK AND JERRY BOCK

Q.: *American musical comedy has had great success not just in America but in the rest of the world. As practitioners of the form, you must have thought a good deal about where it came from and how it developed up to the time when you entered into it. Would you tell us your views?*

HARNICK: Speaking for myself, I have not spent that much time thinking about or studying the origins of American musical comedy; that is a job for the scholar or critic. I am interested in hearing a lot, and particularly these days when summer stock or off-Broadway produces some of the old musicals I run to see them with great curiosity, hoping that they will do them in a style that tries to be close to the original. But as far as going out of my way to study them, I don't do it as a conscious effort.

BOCK: I thoroughly agree with Sheldon in terms of my own experience. It has been more through osmosis, listening to recordings of classical albums, attending the theater not as a separate study so much as an impetus, a stimulus for our own work. I have never been self-conscious of the history of the area of the theater to which we are contributing.

Q.: *For most people the modern American musical begins with* Oklahoma!, *the Rodgers and Hammerstein Western musical, in which there was more of an attempt than had been made in the past to develop character, to see that the music and the dance were more closely related to the atmosphere, to the setting, and to the characters involved in the action. In the older musicals the song was the opportunity for the singer to display his talent, or the dancer to display his particular gift——*

HARNICK: Or for the writer to make the hit parade, which was a big consideration and something that audiences anticipated more than they do now. Everybody likes to hear a good song, but I think our audiences today are more willing to hear material that falls in the category of character songs rather than popular songs.

BOCK: By the way, "musical comedy" is no longer an apt term for what a lot of us are trying to write. I don't know what the correct term is. I know Jerome Robbins sometimes calls it "lyric theater." We don't like to call it a "play with music," because that puts the emphasis on the play part of it with occasional songs, rather than on a piece that is as important musically as it is dramatically.

HARNICK: I kind of like "musical play."

Q.: *If you didn't deliberately study the history of your art before you entered into it, how did you happen to become collaborators in the lyric theater, the musical play?*

HARNICK: I have puzzled many times as to what led me into the theater, because I had almost no interest in it at all until I got out of the Army. I know I always had an interest in writing verse, most predominantly comic verse, because my mother always wrote little poems for occasions in Chicago, where I was born. Every time there was a birthday or anniversary my mother would commemorate it with a poem, so I began to write little poems. Where the mystery comes is that instead of writing sentimental poems I found myself writing poems with strange endings, switch endings, comic poems, as far back as I remember, but why, I don't know. I did that all through grammar school. In high school I met a fellow and we started to write sketches to perform for the students, and started to write parodies. Along with this I had been studying the violin and was thinking of trying to become a professional musician.

Then I went into the Army for three years. There was a volunteer special service unit that some of the fellows put together. I had enough time, so I hung around the theater and began to be used in the sketches, and I decided to try to write a few songs for performance. I wrote a couple of satirical songs about our particular Army life; I met a man there who said he thought I had the talent to do something professionally. I still didn't know anything about theater, and it wasn't until I got out of the Army and went to Northwestern University on the GI Bill that I started to go to theatrical productions. Among other things, the drama group did *The Threepenny Opera* and a revue every year, a student revue. I began to contribute to that, and by the time I got out of Northwestern University I liked the idea of musical theater. At that time the musical theater that I knew was practically all revue; I still wasn't going to many of the downtown Chicago productions, and usually the ones I saw I couldn't enjoy because I could only afford to sit up in the balcony, where I couldn't hear too well; they just kind of went past me.

However, there were two things that influenced me—one was Gilbert and Sullivan, which came very early. Without thinking of making my life in the musical theater, I loved Gilbert and Sullivan. The exuberance of the music and the technical skill with words tickled me; I suppose I have a talent in that field, and there was a rapport between me and what I heard. The other influence was a girl named Charlotte Rae at Northwestern, who later came to New York and entered the theater. She had an album of *Finian's Rainbow;* Charlotte was excited about it and played it for me. I was stunned by it because the notion of the Gilbertian kind of fun with words and at the same time saying something of importance was a marvelous combination. So when I graduated from Northwestern, having contributed to the annual revue every year, I felt this was what I wanted to try to do. I came to New York with the idea that if I could combine the fun of writing lyrics with the importance of trying to say something, it would be marvelous.

Bock: I am very interested to hear Sheldon's story in detail because, of course, during this period unknowingly our paths had crossed, as separated as we were. As far as my mother is concerned, she tells me surely that when I was two years old she sat me in front of an old Majestic radio and I kept perfect rhythm on a toy drum to all the music that came over. No one else was witness, so I can't quite prove it, but maybe that is where my musical inclination started. At any rate I took piano lessons, as many children do, for about four or five years, and during the course of these lessons I found myself composing in a most immature and basic style; I took pieces that I heard and played them by ear, doing very simple variations on their themes. Also I committed to memory far too quickly the pieces that I was supposed to do, and rather than sight-read them accurately I would fill in what my ear told me sounded right.

HARNICK: What we call technically "slopping through."

BOCK: Yes, and my piano teacher would say: "It is quite lovely, but it is not the way Chopin wrote it." When I reached high school I found myself composing a little more, and finally on a war-bond drive the high school did an original musical to raise money for a hospital naval ship—that was the first score I boldly attempted to write. It was a small success in Flushing, New York, but I still wasn't convinced that this was to be my career. As a matter of fact, when I graduated from high school I went to the University of Wisconsin, determined to study journalism. When I went up there during registration week, I had an impulse to audition for the music school. I had no repertory whatsoever because I hadn't studied for five or six years, but I had been playing jazz and popular music during that period. And so I dared to give as my audition piece an arrangement of Army bugle calls in the styles of various composers, attempting to show my classical background as well, ending up with a boogiewoogie version. The professors were rather aghast at this and they said: "Well, Mr. Bock, you show signs of inventiveness, but you must start from the beginning. Are you willing to do so?" And I said yes, and by accident decided to go all the way in a musical career. Then, very briefly after that, I did an original musical at the University of Wisconsin which toured about seven or eight cities in the state and played one night in Chicago.

HARNICK: Where, by a strange coincidence, I *didn't* see it.

BOCK: And then I met somebody at school at Wisconsin and we decided to come East and try our luck as a team. Very fortunately we got work right away in television, writing for Max Liebman on the Sid Caesar and Imogene Coca show. Television at that time was willing to use original musical lyrics. My first Broadway contribution was some numbers in a show called *Catch a Star,* also a revue.

HARNICK: When I came to New York there were a number of revues that were done both on and off-Broadway; I was lucky, and within three or four years I had been able to contribute songs to about four or five revues, usually one song at a time. It was a marvelous opportunity for me to see what happened to a song in front of a paying audience. I wasn't able to support myself too well at it, but at least I was seeing what happened in a theater. At the same time, coming to New York itself was a big influence because I began to go to the theater and to love it. The first book musical I saw may have been *South Pacific,* still playing when I got here, and I was quite overwhelmed by the second act. The first act was so popular I felt as though I knew it and wasn't thrilled, but in the second act, the music was unfamiliar and the whole technique of staging was so fluid and so cinematic that it amazed me. This was not my concept of what you could do on a stage and I was quite drawn to it.

Then there was something else, another parallel between Jerry and me—I had been in New York for about two years when I met a writer named Ira Wallach who had written some satirical books, *Hopalong Freud* and *Hopalong Freud Rides Again.* Ira had a notion for a musical, a satire on the Horatio Alger books. This was the first book musical I attempted, and I learned a lot just from the experience of writing it. I met a producer at a summer resort called Green Mansions, and he wanted to try this musical out up there. This was really the first experience I had of being immersed in a theatrical milieu. They had their own orchestra, their own set designers, their own costumers—and at this point greasepaint entered my blood. I was fascinated with everything that went on around the theater. We put on revues every week. I spent the season at Green Mansions, and for two subsequent seasons I went up there for a few weeks. I know that Jerry had a parallel experience.

BOCK: Yes, it was another version of Green Mansions, a summer resort hotel called Tamiment in Bushkill, Pennsylvania. They had a resident company for the season—a cast, scenic designer, costume designer, sixteen-piece orchestra, conductor, arranger, and writers—and they would do the equivalent of a one-act revue every week. So, in a sense, your assignment was to write and write and write and come up with anywhere from three to five numbers per week, and by the end of the summer you had a catalogue of thirty to fifty songs.

HARNICK: Plus a nervous breakdown.

BOCK: Yes, but I must say, as with Sheldon, that first association with the theater was a very intense one and probably eliminated any doubts that I had about enjoying it and knowing that it was the thing I wanted to do more than anything else. Also, working under pressure like that proved very beneficial. The road tour of a show is comparable to that kind of summer theater where in a very short time you have to solve many problems. Faced with audiences not liking something you have written, and your knowing it and knowing their reasons for disliking it, and therefore having to write another one in a short time—this kind of summer background paid off very well on the road.

HARNICK: This almost takes us up to where we met. I had tried to put a revue together myself, getting sketches from various people, writing some and trying to do the music and lyrics myself. E. Y. Harburg, who still is one of my favorite lyricists, heard my music and advised me to get a composer. I wasn't successful in getting the revue put on. We didn't get the Horatio Alger satire produced. But because of the single songs I had done in various revues I had a small reputation among certain theatrical people, enough so that twice I was called in with shows that were in trouble on the road to try to repair their lyrics. I didn't succeed too well. The important thing for me was that this put me in a laboratory atmosphere. I was able to have what I wrote put on as quickly as possible and see what would happen; the audience were my guinea pigs. One of the shows closed out of town and one of them came back to New York. The latter was *Shangri-La,* and on the opening night after the show I went in to a little bar-restaurant next door and I was introduced to Jerry whose music I had recently heard and liked. Shortly after that we were put together by a producer, Richard Kollmar, who needed a composer and lyricist for a musical comedy called *The Body Beautiful.*

> Q.: *Of course, the theater is a collaborative art, but the lyric theater we have been talking about involves a number of kinds of creative collaboration that legitimate theater (if that isn't an offensive term, too), the straight play, doesn't require. How do you divide responsibility?* Take Fiddler on the Roof. *Where did the idea come from?*

HARNICK: We cannot remember ourselves who suggested it. My memory is that a friend of Jerry's told us to read *Tevye's Daughters.* First we read a different novel of Sholem Aleichem's called——

BOCK: *Wandering Star.*

HARNICK: And we liked it and gave it to Joe Stein, who had written the libretto for *The Body Beautiful.* Joe felt it was far too sprawling a novel to condense for the stage. It just had too many events and was very unfocused and rambling, but it was so rich a novel in many ways it whetted our appetite to read Sholem Aleichem. About that time a friend of ours suggested we read *Tevye's Daughters,* and we loved it. This, by the way, was our fifth musical, and the first time that we had initiated a project. All the other musicals had been submitted to us by producers who had the ideas themselves and set about getting the creative staff to do the work. But Joe Stein, Jerry, and I wrote this one, and when we were far enough along we began to submit it to producers.

In a way *Fiddler on the Roof* is not a good example of divided responsibility because once we got Jerome Robbins he took total responsibility. Whenever Jerome Robbins does a show, he has a complete vision of it which encompasses all of its elements, so that he becomes your boss; he is dictator in the same way Toscanini was, pulling all the elements together, asking the set designer to keep redoing until he comes up with something that is what Jerry wants. He gets into the orchestrations; he gets involved in every conceivable element. A show like *She Loves Me* would be a better example of divided responsibility.

BOCK: *She Loves Me* is an instance of the lyricist and composer and author and director-producer working as a collaborative team in the best sense of the word. A feeling of give and take throughout, a feeling of inspiration throughout, a feeling of group chemistry kept feeding our creative sources. It is a show that we dearly loved doing and one that was, as it always should be, its own reward on opening night. We felt it was a breakthough for us in terms of form and style. And it came about through this choice and ideal collaboration. I think that if you are not willing to be part of a basic give-and-take situation the musical theater can become an unpleasant and unhappy experience. You are obligated to a more complete collaboration in the musical than in any other form.

HARNICK: It requires so much pulling together, and seeing things the same way. If everybody goes into a musical thinking they all see the same way and start working on it and, God forbid, they get on the road and see they are all straining in different directions, the result has to be a hodgepodge. When you think of most artistic creation you think of one man's vision which results in a unified and homogeneous work; it is very hard to achieve that in a musical. You have to have people who are sympathetic to one another and willing to give and take a bit but still not just give in altogether on any point. Usually there is one man who has to be in a position of authority. In *She Loves Me* we had an interesting situation because our producer, Harold Prince, was also directing, and Hal was very conscious of the fact that he was the producer and he leaned over backwards never to say, "Look, fellows, I am the producer and you have got to do it this way, because." Also the director leaned over backwards, and managed by tact and humor and persuasion to keep things going along a certain line.

BOCK: Of course, as director, when a new scene was written and he suddenly realized he had to order a new piece of scenery to be built, all he could do was to talk to himself. Happily the director always won.

Q.: *In general, is it true that the libretto comes first? Do you try to start from a complete libretto?*

BOCK: Yes. The early musicals might be cited as differing from contemporary musicals in that the score was the paramount thing. I have heard that very often a series of songs would be written with a basic outline, very sketchy, and the book became the continuity between the songs. It was a stepchild in the most obvious way.

Q.: *Setting up the music?*

BOCK: Yes. That began to change with plays like *Oklahoma!*, where the materials began to fuse; suddenly just the score wasn't the only important thing. There is a long way to go along those lines. Eventually the book and the score will fuse in such a way that you may not know where one begins and the other ends. I know Sheldon and I feel very strongly about the book being a basic support for the piece that we are writing.

Q.: *If it is true that a more integrated work is what the theater is aiming for, why do librettists tend to go back to novels and to plays for their stories? I should think that to create an original story to be told in song and dance would result in a more integrated work.*

HARNICK: Well, we've thought a lot about that and one reason for that—but not the only one—is the Broadway theater. The musical theater is very expensive to produce and very expensive to run, and many producers and writers are looking for proved property that has succeeded on the stage or has at least the virtue of a household name. They then try to turn it into a musical, thinking that part of the work is already done; if it is a play, there is already a basic script that has been successful on the stage; if a novel, it may have a name presumably worth money at the box office.

BOCK: Or a movie.

HARNICK: Or a movie. There is nothing wrong with this per se. I tend to object to the ransacking of very recent Broadway plays to turn them into musicals within four or five years of their commercial success as plays. This is the theater feeding on itself, and I don't particularly like it. There is another problem for a team that has had to depend on librettists. Television and movies seem to have gathered to themselves a lot of the better writers. The theater is so chancy that a lot of men would prefer to write for the other media. The cry of all songwriters is, Where is the book writer, where is the book writer?

BOCK: Remembering the plays we have done, the first was *The Body Beautiful,* an original story—our least successful. The second one, *Fiorello,* is a hybrid. We had the history of the man and knowledge of his life, but there was no play about him, no formal written document about him. To start us off, it was researched by the author Jerome Weidman and constructed into a musical play by him. *Tenderloin* was based loosely on a novel, and *She Loves Me* was based on a movie which we vaguely remembered. When we saw it again we were enchanted and inspired in terms of making a musical contribution to this romantic play. It was also an impetus for us because we longed to do a love story. *Fiddler* was a series of short stories. Our smorgasbord kind of source for all these pieces, I think, is evidence that a good play might come from any number of sources, and to insist that it comes from originals only, adaptations only, is probably wrong.

HARNICK: Thinking about writers we know, writers only of plays, a kind of analogy comes to me. I have a friend, a painter, and I asked him if he had ever done any sets for the theater. He said no, that he had considered it, but when he thought about having his work be the background for something else his pride got in the way. So that's when I think of men like Arthur Miller and Tennessee Williams and Thornton Wilder: if they don't feel they have the capability of writing lyrics, as a matter of pride they would not want to take collaborators; they are capable of writing something that they can control from start to finish. So it is an unusual writer who sets out to write something that is going to need the work of other people to complete it. Because we are songwriters and need that source, we will seek people out and ask them if they will write librettos.

Q.: *Do skilled librettists, such as Stein, for example, write specifically to create opportunities for music, or do they give you a play?*

BOCK: I think both. That is where the collaboration of the creators comes in. We have many, many conferences, which go unnoticed by everyone but ourselves and which are the fundamental breaking-ground for the day when we will all say, "Okay, we will separate and write," or, "You go home and write and call us in two weeks or two months, when you think there are three scenes or four scenes ready for our contribution." But the work begins as a triumvirate and ends as a triumvirate. It is only during the practical working out that the librettist is not in the same room with us when writing. We are in constant spiritual contact at all times.

HARNICK: The librettists whom we have worked with, with one exception, have all followed this same procedure. They will write a scene and put, in parenthesis, that there could be a song at such a point about such and such a subject, but they always say, "This is just a suggestion," or, "The song will come in another place in the scene," or, "If you don't want to use my suggestion feel free not to." The one exception was in *She Loves Me,* where Joe Masteroff, the playwright, had never written a musical before and what we asked him to do was kind of an experiment all the way around. He was to write a play and let us search through the scenes and find the emotional moments or comic moments which we thought could be well expressed in song, and that is the way we did it. I don't think Joe ever wrote in a scene that there should be a song there. And, as a matter of fact, it was lovely that he wanted this. He wished us to take over into music as much of his finished dialogue as we could, because he felt this would make something different for the musical theater. He wrote in such a way that we ended up with twenty or twenty-one "songs," not all being complete songs but sometimes fragmentary musical moments. But whenever we could, we translated his dialogue into music, a different and very refreshing experience.

Q.: *Now for the question you are constantly asked: Which comes first, the lyrics or the music when you come to your particular contribution?*

HARNICK: Well, it varies with different teams, and I suppose even with people who write both lyrics and music, but we have evolved a kind of standard way of working.

BOCK: Which is totally unpredictable.

HARNICK: When we know what the book is about, what period it concerns, who the people are, what the locality is, etc., and what the tone of the work is, while I am studying that and thinking of ideas for songs, usually before I have begun a lyric, Jerry begins to write musical material. When he reaches the point of having composed anywhere from ten to twenty pieces, he will put them on tape and give me the tape to take home to listen to. Usually there are a number of things on the tape that I find so exciting musically I can't wait to put words to them so I can sing them. If anything on the tape strikes me as being very right for a particular idea I have, then I will plunge in and start that way. But in every show we have done it is just accidental that by the time the show is finished about 50 per cent of the lyrics came first, because when I find that I have an idea for a song and there is nothing on tape that seems to fit the notion, I will start a lyric and give it to Jerry, and he will take over from there. It goes back and forth. We work both ways.

BOCK: That tape, by the way, comes from the same source from which Sheldon works. It is based on the discussions we had previously and perhaps from having read some scenes from the first-act outline. What I base the music on is not just pure guesswork but a beginning feeling of character and atmosphere and the environment of the play and the people. I try to translate that musically.

147

Q.: *I know that both of you are up to your neck in creative activities right now. What is your next project?*

HARNICK: Well, we are working on a musical which we are having great fun with because it has a lot of challenges. It is an evening of three one-act musicals. The musicals themselves are based on separate stories, but they have an underlying connection, even though the three stories are by different writers.

Floating around in my head are a number of things that this whole discussion has brought up. One is opera, because we talk about Rodgers and Hammerstein as being a point of departure in the American musical theater, yet, of course, their works didn't spring full-blown from their own heads. *Porgy and Bess* and *Showboat* and various other productions must have influenced them. When we talk about music, the integrated musical theater, then, of course, we realize there is nothing new about that because opera integrated music and characters, although it is not particularly an American form. It was Rodgers and Hammerstein and other men who introduced jazz elements and popular elements into this kind of hybrid integrated form. Something we hope is new is the idea of taking a subject, making the characters three-dimensional people, not relying solely on jokes or block comedy scenes or flashy production numbers to tell our story. A better way to put it is this: to try and tell a story that has some substance to it and to tell it in terms of three-dimensional characters and song and dance. So what we are working on now is closer to opera in a way, at least one or two of the pieces will be predominantly musical. One of the problems with opera is what to do with the material that you cannot set as arias or as lyrics or passionate moments. In the old days they solved that by making recitatives. We don't have to do that, because in our form we can go back to dialogue. We can say, Why sing it? We will allow for music in all the important moments, while moments of exposition or of chatter can be spoken.

BOCK: Yes, it is really the best of both possible worlds. Although we are thinking to express ourselves more musically than ever before, we are not obligated to do it without exception. Sheldon

148

and I share the view that when contemporary operas are based on severe rules and regulations of tradition, attempting to translate chatter or conversation into musical terms, they are artificial, untrue. To let speech happen frequently and to do the rest in music might be the combination that will define a future kind of musical play. We are anxious to work in this field more and more.

HARNICK: It has already been attempted with *Porgy and Bess* and with Frank Loesser's musical *The Most Happy Fella*. First of all, you must find a work that has such emotional substance that it will benefit by the use of music.

Q.: *But it doesn't have to have a musical subject in the literal sense. You don't have to have musical characters?*

HARNICK: No, as a matter of fact I was asked to write a piece for the California theater program of *Fiddler on the Roof* and I chose to write about something which was very close to me and to Jerry. Whenever you start to write a project in which somebody figures who is known to the audience, as Tevye is known as a comic-tragic figure, some people will ask how he can sing. That always bothers me because we feel any character can sing on stage if his motivation makes him reach an emotional point where the emotions will pour out; singing is almost more natural than speaking.

Q.: *In the older theater this would be simpler. In the nineteenth-century theater actors acted rhetorically, whereas today actors are trained to talk to their T shirts and scratch their collars to express their emotions. You may have a real contribution to make in enlarging the whole theater, not just musical theater. What do you think about taking people who are known primarily as actors and putting them in musical roles?*

BOCK: We love it. I know in our auditions we more and more look first for the actor and then hope he's musical. Even by musical, we don't mean perfectly pear-shaped tones, we mean fundamental sense of rhythm and pitch, because as an actor he can give a performance of a song that may be of greater value and focus less on the separation of song and talk as many singers might do. It is another aspect of integration; hopefully it should be all of a piece, and the audience ought not to be startled when that actor opens his mouth and sings.

HARNICK: We have had great fun and great satisfaction with people like Howard DaSilva and Barbara Baxley, Zero Mostel and Herschel Bernardi, Luther Adler, Jack Warden, and Tom Bosley, all actors who have a good sense of rhythm. When they sing it is not a sound that makes your toes curl. There are people whom we have auditioned and didn't want to use; when they opened their mouths what came out was unpleasant to hear even though they had a sense of pitch and rhythm.

BOCK: They were toe-curlers.

Q.: *You profess not to be historical, but you are going back to three of the great works of the musical theater, all of which were either written for the legitimate actors or performed that way.* The Beggar's Opera, *the first English musical comedy, was written for actors and played by actors.* Knickerbocker Holiday *was written for and performed by Walter Huston. And most recently was the great success of Rex Harrison in* My Fair Lady.

BOCK: And it is really magic when it works as with Harrison who was obviously musical. He may have sung-spoken those songs, but he did it with deftness and accuracy and, most important, with a performance that was so integrated and so unified that it was a remarkable achievement.

Q.: *Can we have an American opera as long as we don't insist on* bel canto?

BOCK: So long as we don't insist on calling it opera.

HARNICK: Now we are back to where we started with that term; my own favorite is "musical theater."

Q.: *I always thought opera meant a total work, one in which every element, whether spoken or sung or danced, was integrated into the unit. Isn't this very much what you fellows have in mind?*

BOCK: Yes.

HARNICK: While on the subject of nomenclature, there is the

problem of that terrible expression "serious music." Whatever Jerry and I write is deadly serious. Hopefully it comes out popular but not just popular. I would like to find a better term for it than "serious music," but I can't think of one.

BOCK: Do you mean by serious music classical, as opposed to frivolous, music?

HARNICK: For instance, symphonic music contrasted with dance-band music.

BOCK: Yes, but the term "serious music" would always be associated with symphonic music, although jazz today can be very serious and work very well in the theater.

Q.: *You are part of a large group. Most people who write comedy, who have the comic view of life, are ultimately very serious people indeed, but nobody describes* The Importance of Being Earnest *as a serious play. They may make condescending remarks about* You Can't Take It with You, *and George S. Kaufman was a comedian, but he was a very serious man who expressed himself in this particular way. Isn't the comic view of life just as serious ultimately as the tragic view of life?*

BOCK: Yes, and surely as difficult to create.

Q.: *Maybe more difficult, since so much depends on style rather than emotion. Perhaps the term you are looking for is "organic music," something which has a functional part in the total?*

HARNICK: No. I find myself going back to musicals, musical theater, and thinking about other kinds of musicals like *Hello, Dolly!* From the nature of this discussion I wouldn't want to give the idea that everyone of us in the musical theater is traveling the same path. There are many people who are looking for things to write for the theater which will be no more nor less than good entertainment. I think it is safe to say that even there the influence of the last twenty years has taken root, even the entertainments are more integrated than they were twenty or twenty-five years ago.

Q.: *This may be one of the reasons for the death of the*

revue. The audiences want a more integrated experience, don't they?

BOCK: I think they have come to appreciate that and are less willing to accept a totally lightweight book as an excuse to get into some songs. But there are always exceptions. A company like *Beyond the Fringe* comes over and captivates us enormously, and *Wait a Minim!*, which is a revue. But even they have larger responsibilities. And I think the people are coming to want that.

PART IV

Off-Broadway

13 THE NONCOMMERCIAL THEATER IN NEW YORK

Bernard F. Dukore

To many people the American theater means Broadway, and Broadway has become associated with neon signs and phony glitter, with the opulence and gaudiness that masks shallowness or emptiness. In short, Broadway means the commercial theater, and the Broadway theaters are the *boulevard* theaters of New York City, the theatrical capital of the United States.

But there is an alternative, off-Broadway. Although most of the off-Broadway theaters are in New York's Greenwich Village or on the Lower East Side, off-Broadway is not so much a matter of location as it is a state of mind. If Broadway evokes images of shallowness, sugariness, and superficial slickness, then off-Broadway brings to mind the image of the dedicated artist in the loft. If Broadway is commercialdom, then off-Broadway is anti-commercialdom.

However, these contrasts that I have indicated are not rigid compartments; they are generalizations and, as is the case with all generalizations, exceptions can be found. We should not forget that Broadway has presented plays by Bernard Shaw, Bertolt Brecht, Albert Camus, and Jean-Paul Sartre; nor should we forget that off-Broadway has presented plays by Maxwell Anderson, Agatha Christie, Cole Porter, and Tennessee Williams. When we find stars whose names have great commercial value—such as Shelley Winters, Eli Wallach, and Franchot Tone—performing off-Broadway, the lines separating the two become blurred.

This does not mean that there are no differences; the general points of contrast still hold. Definitions are based on the center, not on the edges. Usually, off-Broadway produces the avant-garde playwrights while Broadway produces the derrière-garde. Since the financial failure of *Waiting for Godot* on Broadway, Samuel Beckett's New York address has been off-Broadway. By and large, this has been the New York address of Ionesco, Pinter, and Genet as well. Ionesco's *Rhinoceros* was presented on Broadway, but this play is his most conventional and therefore most commercial comedy. Harold Pinter's *The Caretaker* was presented on Broadway, but this was the importation of a London hit, with the London cast intact. Jean Genet has yet to move to "respectable" Broadway. When the avant-garde gets to Broadway, it is either an internationally famous play that is thought to have sufficient snob appeal to be successful, a not particularly avant-garde play by an avant-garde playwright, or an importation of a London success. Also, off-Broadway is more congenial to the one-act play. A bill of one-act plays on Broadway is a rare occasion; such programs are considered death at the box office. Production costs are lower off-Broadway, and producers are more willing to take risks. This may account in part for the presentation of European avant-garde playwrights off-Broadway; these dramatists often tend to write short rather than long plays. Off-Broadway, too, is the home of the revival: Euripides, Aristophanes, Marlowe, Ford, Chekhov, Ibsen, Pirandello. When there is a revival on Broadway, it is either an import from England or a star vehicle or both.

But are there native off-Broadway playwrights? Do they form a "school" or at least a trend? Although it sometimes seems that the only "school" they represent is that of American individualism, with each dramatist firmly determined to be as unlike any of his fellows as he possibly can, nevertheless several clusters may be seen.

There are, to begin with, the traditonal playwrights. William Hanley's one-act play *Mrs. Dally Has a Lover* is a sensitive story of a thirty-eight-year-old married woman and her eighteen-year-old lover; its curtain-raiser, *Whisper into My Good Ear,* is a tale of two lonely old men in a park—one nearly blind, the other homosexual—who find friendship on the brink of death. Murray Schisgal's *The Typists* presents a male and a female typist growing older in one uninterrupted act and is a vehicle for two star actors; its curtain-raiser, *The Tiger,* is a comic yarn about a sex-starved abductor whose victim finds him sufficiently interesting to have, on her own volition, an affair with him. All four of these plays are competent, craftsmanlike pieces of work by playwrights of professional caliber. But they are not at all different from the usual Broadway product—except for the fact that they are one-act plays; hence, I suspect, their production off-Broadway. Jack Richardson's *The Prodigal* is a retelling of the *Oresteia,* in which circumstances rather than free will force Orestes to abandon his intellectual detachment and avenge a father who has been a stranger to him and to espouse a cause he despises. Although *The Prodigal* is a remarkably adult play, its dramaturgy is conventional. However, a "Greek play" by an unknown author is too much of a risk for Broadway; thus, off-Broadway. Then there is Edward Albee, the United States' most praised recent playwright. *The Zoo Story* (his first and probably his best play) is a perfectly conventional, realistic, psychological drama. It is also a one-acter, and so it was left to off-Broadway to "discover" him on a double bill with *Krapp's Last Tape,* by Samuel Beckett. Albee left realism for a while with his obvious and obviously derivative *The American Dream* and *Sandbox,* but he abandoned the nonrealistic mode and made his Broadway debut with—and I do not think this is coincidental—his first full-length play, the traditionally realistic *Who's Afraid of Virginia Woolf?*

Several of our young playwrights thumb their noses at realism. James Dey, for example, in *The Redemptor,* an Ionesco-like parable about The Bomb—written, I must add, before he had read a word of Ionesco's—spins a story of an ancient scientist named Julius Apocalypse who, with his wife, Albatross, lives in a latter-day version of an ivory tower: the thirty-seventh floor of a walk-up tenement in New York City. Apocalypse has invented a bomb which will blow up the entire world—not part of it but all of it. He is anxious to demonstrate his invention before someone else beats him to it and secures all of the credit. At the end of the play, he and his wife stand lovingly together, their fingers in their ears; as she sweetly coos, "Goodbye, love. And congratulations," he blows up the world. The absurdly elephantine title *Oh Dad, Poor Dad, Mamma's Hung You in the Closet and I'm Feelin' So Sad* is appropriate for a grotesque satire on American moms, featuring a Philip Wylie monster mother, a frightened son who has been prevented from maturing, a pretty girl who unsuccessfully tries to remedy this lack, and a stuffed corpse (the "Poor Dad" of the title) who falls out of the bedroom closet onto the bodies of the boy and girl at an extremely inconvenient moment. However, *Oh Dad, Poor Dad* is at the same time a parody on French avant-garde drama. One of the difficulties with the play, I think, is that Kopit has not adequately connected the serious satire on Momism and the playful spoof on the avant-garde.

So far, the new American playwrights of the off-Broadway scene appear to be either minor-league players trying to crack the majors uptown (and sometimes succeeding) or bedfellows of the School of Paris. But there is another group of playwrights whose work fits into neither of these categories and who seem to have achieved a uniquely American identity; they are loosely bound by a common desire to portray realistically the reality they see around them, by a common dissatisfaction with the techniques of the commercial play, and by similar experimentation with new techniques. I would like to concentrate on what appears to be the significant works of these playwrights—Jack Gelber's *The Connection*, Kenneth Brown's *The Brig*, and LeRoi Jones's *Dutchman*. These plays comprise what might be called the New Realism, for although they are realistic plays, they are different from the realism of Ibsen, Hauptmann, Chayefsky, and Wesker.

The Connection is a play about dope addicts. Usually, this sort of drama is either a tale of a courageous junkie who kicks the habit (substitute the word "booze" for the word "pot" and you can easily see the kinship with the melodramas of yesteryear) or else a psychological study of human frailty which pleads for compassionate understanding. For Gelber, both of these approaches are "square," and he satirizes the old-fashioned drama when one of his characters assures the audience that *The Connection* does not conclude—as, by the way, *A Hatful of Rain* does—with a housewife calling the police and asking them to come immediately to the theater because her husband is a junkie. Gelber uses narcotics addiction as a metaphor for that connection which we all need to enable us to go on living. There are no basic differences between the junkies we see on stage waiting for their connection to arrive and give them a fix and the respectable people in the audience who probably have a legal and more socially acceptable connection. The man who arrives with the narcotics, Cowboy (so named, I suppose, because he comes with "horse"), reminds one of the addict who has condemned the "daytime" people for being "square" and not "hip," that there is nothing wrong with having a day job, that there are good and bad hipsters as well as good and bad squares, and that although he could not tolerate a daily work job since he prefers his hours as they are, this does not make him better than the daytime people. Neither, it is implied, does it make him essentially *different* from the daytime people. Some people need a vitamin pill, others a new coat, a new car, reassurance from an analyst, or reassurance from a minister—there are numerous socially approved connections. As Solly, the wise (Solomon-like) junkie, puts it, each fix that we wait for, that we desperately need, whatever that fix may be, is "A fix of hope. A fix to forget. A fix to remember, to be sad, to be happy, to be, to be." We all, Gelber is saying, take some form of dope.

It is society's unwillingness to acknowledge this, and to condemn or—what is in some respects worse—to condescendingly pity the narcotics addicts, that constitutes one of Gelber's major themes and certainly his major accusation. In addition to Cowboy's ironic condescension to *us* in the passage I have paraphrased, there are characters in the play who represent the respectable world; moreover, that world is actually present in the auditorium. During the course of the play, two of the representatives of the world of respectability are drawn into the world of the drug addicts. By having them take dope, Gelber dramatizes the bond between both worlds. But Gelber is also concerned with the actual members of the respectable world, the audience.

As we enter the auditorium we see that the curtain is already up. The realistic stage setting looks as though it needs to be disinfected. There are people in that setting, we notice. Actors? Or are they bums who have wandered in from the street? Of course they must be actors. But they too appear to be in need of fumigation. They recline on a bed or are slumped over a table or wander about aimlessly. One of them plays a few bars on a piano or beats a snare drum a few times, then gives it up as a worthless activity. One of them occasionally—but only occasionally—glances at us as if we were a necessary evil to be tolerated. Another furtively peeks at us, then looks away with loathing. We begin to feel uncomfortable. The performance, we realize later (some of us realize now), has already begun, and we are in it. A "producer" appears, welcomes us to the theater, and introduces the "author" of the evening's entertainment. He speaks to us in language that reveals him as the square trying to be hip, and some of us feel still more uncomfortable, for this is our language. He tells us that the author (named Jaybird, an appropriate tag for this foolish, gullible young man) has lived among dope addicts for a few months in order to understand them. We learn, too, that Jaybird has written character biographies and some form of scenario for what will be an improvised performance. We are told smilingly that this improvisation will be performed by real dope addicts, whose payment for the evening's entertainment will be, we are also told smilingly, a fix. In order to calm the more apprehensive members of the audience before we enter the lobby during the interval, the producer assures us that this fix—to be given during the second act—will be "a scientifically accurate amount of heroin." The discomfort we felt at the beginning of the performance is intensified. If these are real addicts assembled for our amusement, what does that make us, who pay for this sort of amusement? If they are to be turned on, what does that make us, who pay for the dose? We are not allowed to forget this. On a few occasions—just enough to make us remember—we are reminded of this explicitly. In the first act one of the junkies, waiting for Cowboy to arrive with the heroin, savagely indicts the audience, "I really don't believe any of you understand what this is about. You're stupid. Why are you here? Because you want to see someone suffer. You want to laugh at me? You don't want to know me." And in the second act, after Cowboy has arrived, another junkie, who has just been turned on, tells us in a more jovial manner, "I want to take the opportunity to thank each and every kind, gentle, and good contributor in the audience. You have helped a most noble cause, and a cause that is dear to our hearts. That goodness, that goodness that flows in our veins is the evidence—is the evidence of our gratitude toward you and every one of our fellow men."

The pattern of the play is straightforward: in the first act, the addicts wait for Cowboy to bring the dope. Just before the act ends he is seen through the window. During the second act, the junkies are turned on. One of them, who has not received his "kick" from the drug, gives himself a second fix (on stage!) that proves to be an overdose and that almost kills him. Also during the second act, the playwright and one of two cameramen who have arrived to film the event are persuaded to get a fix. These two—who have been sitting in our midst in the auditorium during most of the action—establish the physical link between our world and the world of the junkies. As Jaybird himself puts it at the end of the play, "Well, if it wasn't junk, I would have been involved with something else."

I call Gelber's play an example of the New Realism. I do not do so because he uses a group of social outcasts to symbolize social incasts; after all, Gorky did this in *The Lower Depths*. Nor do I use the term because he is leveling an attack upon his audience; Shaw did this in *Mrs. Warren's Profession*. One of the things that makes Gelber's play so unique as realism is that he uses so many devices of the nonrealistic theater. Consider: the "author" is introduced to the audience; the "producer" tells us that what we will see has no naturalistic basis; a character enters and asks whether the play has begun; actors go into the auditorium and later return to the stage; the "producer" stops the action of the play to introduce the cast to the audience; the "author" complains that the actors are not following his story and has an argument with them; several characters address us directly; one character announces that he will panhandle from us during the interval, and he does, etc. If these devices remind us of anyone, they remind us not of any of the naturalistic playwrights but of Pirandello! And Gelber's practice is indeed Pirandellian. He audaciously—and successfully, I think—uses theatricality to make us believe that we are watching reality. In *The Connection,* the basic setup is not actors who are going to play junkies, but junkies who are going to try to be actors. Therefore, whenever we are reminded that we are in a theater looking at a stage, we are at the same time reminded that we are looking at non-actors. The theatricalism enforces the realism to create a slice of life that is much more successful than might have been achieved if Gelber had tried "straight" realism. Gelber directs his audience's attention to the unreality he wants them to focus on in order to divert their attention from the unreality he wants to hide: namely, that actors are playing junkies playing actors.

Kenneth Tynan called *The Connection* the most exciting new American play produced off-Broadway since World War II. I agree, and it is mainly because of Gelber's remarkable accomplishment that I have devoted so much space to this play. The other major plays of the New Realism that I am going to discuss —*The Brig* and *Dutchman*—are, I think, important but less successful.

The Brig, a grim enactment of life in a Marine Corps prison written by an ex-marine, Kenneth Brown, uses none of the theatricalist devices of *The Connection.* Heavy chicken-wire separates the stage from the audience. The audience stays on its side of the chicken-wire, the actors on theirs. The play has no plot. It is a series of six scenes comprising a typical day in a Marine Corps prison, beginning at 4:00 A.M., shortly before the prisoners are officially awakened, and ending with "Lights out." During this typical day, we are exposed to the brutality and bestiality of life in the brig. Prisoners are designated, not by a name but by a number, or else they are called "maggots" and "worms." Prisoners are not allowed to walk but must run or trot. Before doing or saying anything, they must loudly request permission to do or say it: "Sir, prisoner number ten"—or whatever his number is—"requests permission to speak, sir." If the prisoner adds "please," he is reprimanded and made to repeat his request. If the guard does not think the request was made in a sufficiently loud voice, he demands that it be repeated until the decibels satisfy him. A white line marks every entrance and exit—between the cells and the corridor, between one corridor and another, between the turnkey's area and the compound, etc. Whenever a prisoner wishes to cross a white line he must request permission to do so. If he crosses without permission, he is beaten. In fact, he may be beaten at any time and for any reason at all.

These beatings are a constantly recurring feature of life in the brig. Here is a typical example. Sease, one of the guards, calls to a prisoner who is about to distribute shovels to four other prisoners.

SEASE: Nineteen, you crossed my white line without asking me first. Tonight is your night, nineteen.
Sease gets up and walks to Nineteen.
SEASE: Now give each worm his shovel.
Nineteen hands a shovel to each prisoner.
Sease punches Nineteen in the stomach.
SEASE: Tonight is your night, nineteen.
Pause.
SEASE: Get out, maggots.
The four Prisoners disappear . . .

The repeated beatings, the references to human beings as numbers or as maggots, the incessant requests for permission to cross white lines—these accumulate into steadily mounting images of humanity dehumanized and subhumanized. They reach a terrifying emotional climax when one of the prisoners cracks up, shouts that his name is not twenty-six but James Turner, and is put into

163

a strait jacket and removed. Following this scene, however, is the quieter but more frightening final episode: a new prisoner is brought in and is shown the ropes. The pattern repeats itself.

More is involved than a cumulative series of scenes in a torture factory. First, the picture is an accurate one. Second, as with *The Connection,* we are indicted and are made acutely uncomfortable by the spectacle. If this is dehumanized life, then we, who tolerate or are silent in the face of such barbarism, are even more inhuman than the guards in the play. In addition, again as with *The Connection,* the events on stage serve as metaphor for a larger issue. We, too, Brown seems to imply, exist in an insecure and often totalitarian world in which the sky can come crashing down on us and we can be destroyed by the most minor infraction of totally arbitrary rules. Finally, the play achieves a direct, non-literary, kinesthetic communication with us. Not only does the violence affect our very muscles, but the repetition of phrases, of sentences, of movements, and of the violence itself creates an insinuating rhythm that provokes a direct experience of the cruelty that occurs onstage.

This is more than documentary realism, though it is also that. The very pulse of the play is transmitted to the audience. Another aspect of this New Realism that distinguishes it from the older type is the abandonment of traditional features of play construction. Indeed, some have called *The Brig* not a play at all but a literal re-enactment of military prison life. Although it is true that *The Brig* does not have a plot, but instead has a group of incidents related by a common theme, locale, and characters, it is not a literal re-enactment; instead it is a series of scenes whose basic rhythms are repeated and built in such a way as to force a direct, kinesthetic response from the audience.

In terms of the rejection of conventional dramaturgy, the use of a cycle to suggest recurrence and deadly inevitability, the attack upon the audience linked with a direct assault upon its senses and emotions, the presentation of an unsavory segment of American life, and the use of this segment to serve as metaphor for a larger area not only of American life but of Western life, *The Brig* appears to be following the general lines of *The Connection. Dutchman,* by the Negro poet LeRoi Jones, also appears to follow these general lines.

Dutchman, whose title may be an ironic reference to the Wagnerian opera, is a one-act paean of hate. A thirty-year-old, sexy, neurotic white woman gets on a subway train, sits next to a twenty-year-old Negro, and gives him what looks like a come-on. She alternately speaks seductively to him, ignores him, grabs his thigh, and insults him. One begins to wonder—along with the Negro boy—whether she is quite sane. At one moment she looks him in the eye and talks of unbuttoning her dress and letting her skirt fall; the next moment she calls him a "black nigger." The boy is embarrassed and does not know what to make of her strange behavior, but at the same time he is reluctant to pass up what looks like a wild evening. Her overtures become more obviously erotic: she sings, dances, tries to persuade him to dance with her, and finally calls on him to make love to her right then and there. His refusal prompts a violent reaction. She mocks him, curses him, and tries to humiliate him. As she taunts him, the other subway riders laugh. The Negro, provoked at last, thrusts her into her seat and slaps her to shut her up. Then, in a flood of rhetorical venom, he pours out the hatred he has for her and every white. His white man's three-button suit, he says, is a disguise to keep him from cutting the white man's throat; the white man does not know that Bessie Smith and Charlie Parker—whom he idolizes—hated him, that Bessie sang and Bird played in order to hide their hate, and that these very performances became acts of hate. In the heart of every Negro, he tells her, is hatred for every white, and this hatred will one day become murder. She then takes out a knife and stabs him. She orders the other riders to throw his body out of the train and to get off at the next stop. They obey. She scribbles a note in a notebook. Another twenty-year-old Negro enters. She looks at him provocatively. Curtain.

Dutchman might be described as a realistic play with the motivation left out. This is one element which distinguishes it from traditionally realistic plays. For Jones, what the white woman does is more important than why she does it. Although her actions are believable, her motivation is not spelled out. Antonin Artaud, spokesman for a theater that would create subliminal shocks and that would forcefully convey to the spectators a sense of the cruelty of existence, wanted the theatrical experience to leave an ineffaceable scar. LeRoi Jones, by concentrating on the social attitudes and actions created by unstated motivations, and at the same time making the sensuality and violence a direct sensory and emotional experience, goes at least some distance toward realizing that aim. *Dutchman* may not leave an ineffaceable scar —far from it!—but it does create a considerable shock. This may be said not only of *Dutchman* but also of *The Brig* and *The Connection*. All three plays blend an attack on the values of the audience with an attack on its senses and emotions in order to create a direct theatrical experience.

From the unadorned dialogue of Samuel Beckett to the almost baroque splendor of Jean Genet's language, European playwrights are creating various dramatic visions which constitute what Martin Esslin has called "the theater of the absurd." The major experimental playwrights of the United States are pursuing their own visions and do not, in the main, appear to be tormented by "the absurdity of the human condition." This may be a blessing, for the concept has become a cliché. Nevertheless, they are responding to the cruelty of existence as they see it inside themselves and as they find it reflected in the world around them at a particular moment of history—Jones, showing the tensions of the Negro in the white man's world; Brown, portraying the inhumanity of a totalitarian system; Gelber, presenting man lost and alone, trying to make a connection with something which, if it will not give his life meaning, will at least enable him to go on living. John Osborne's febrile protagonist of *Look Back in Anger*, Jimmy Porter, complains at one point that he is living in the American Age. Whether or not this is cause for complaint depends upon one's point of view. But in many respects Jimmy

Porter is right, and whatever one's point of view may be, our major experimental playwrights, in presenting dramatic images of the fears and tensions of their world, are speaking out not only for a vital segment of the United States but for a vital segment of the rest of the Western world as well.

14 THE PROFESSIONAL THEATER AND THE UNIVERSITIES

Arthur Lithgow

A recent National Economic Review published by *The New York Times* reveals that the "arts market" is one of the fastest growing markets in the United States today. "Consumer spending on the arts rose from 1953 to 1960 by about 130 per cent. By the early nineteen-seventies the arts market is expected to amount to $7 billion dollars a year," money spent in museums, symphony halls and playhouses, and for classical records and literature. "The cultural ferment is generating the construction of theatres and multipurpose arts buildings. About 1,000 will be built in the United States in the next decade at a cost of $4 billion."

Most of these structures will be built within the expansion plans of colleges and universities, and many of them will house professional programs performed by established artists with or without the participation of graduate or undergraduate students of the performing arts.

These statistics are the more remarkable when we reflect that there was a time within living memory when there were no speech and drama departments on the campuses of American colleges. Speech departments are the relatively recent outgrowths of the old, more academic, and venerable departments of rhetoric, and the speech and drama professors today are the former students of such men as John Dolman, A. M. Drummond, and E. C. Mabie, who pioneered the establishment of drama departments at the Universities of Pennsylvania, Cornell, and Iowa, respectively. From the university platforms of professors of rhetoric to theater platforms for professional players has been a development of three teaching generations.

By all odds the best publicized of the associations between professional performers and American universities is that of the organization known as APA, or Association of Producing Artists, which first performed in repertory at the Phoenix Theatre off-Broadway, in New York, and with the sponsorship of the Phoenix producers, T. Edward Hambleton and Norris Houghton. In 1966 the company moved to the Lyceum Theatre on Broadway, and the group is now called the APA-Phoenix. Publicity attendant upon New York City performances has resulted in the widespread knowledge that APA performed for three seasons with the Professional Arts program of the University of Michigan, with alternating seasons in New York.

The resourceful young actor-director-producer of APA-Phoenix, Ellis Rabb, most graphically characterizes the step-by-step developments which have brought the professional theater and the American university into close and productive association. His productions of *Man and Superman, Judith, War and Peace,* and *You Can't Take It with You* in New York are the culmination of more than fifteen years of skills, training, growth, inspiration, and investments of his own and his professional associates and the investments and resources, besides those of the Phoenix and Lyceum theaters, of Carnegie Institute of Technology, Wellesley College, Antioch College, Princeton University, and the University of Michigan.

Since it was my privilege to select Ellis Rabb in an audition when he was a student in the Carnegie Tech drama department in 1952, and since I wrote his first professional contract with the Antioch College Shakespeare Festival of those days, I suggest that Rabb's progress, which I have watched with close attention and friendship, is a case history of the growth of the American repertory movement and its close connection with the American campus.

In 1952, Antioch College was prepared to launch an ambitious plan for an annual Festival of Shakespearean Plays to be presented on an outdoor platform constructed in front of Antioch's administration building during the summer months. I served as the general director of the undertaking, and it was my early task to begin seeking skilled young performers to undertake the major acting chores. It was well known at that time that the professional training program in the drama department of Carnegie Tech was turning out a generation of performers of the classics, particularly under the influence of its "Styles in Acting" course taught by Henry Boettcher, Allen Fletcher, and Mary Morris.

In early spring of that year I went to Pittsburgh to attend a performance of *Hamlet,* directed by Mr. Boettcher, with an eye for the talented young man playing the leading role. As it turned out I engaged a vital young performer enacting the role of the Player King. He seems to have been just what the Antioch College Shakespeare Festival was looking for; he played a great variety of roles that season, making a considerable impact on the audience and in no small measure contributing to the success of that crucial first season. This was the launching of Ellis Rabb's professional career.

Ellis Rabb had already served his apprenticeship on a college campus. The summer before his coming to Antioch he had been one of the younger members of the company sponsored by Wellesley College in a summer classical theater season which shortly became known as "Group 20" under the management of Alison Ridley Evans; after half a dozen summer seasons at Antioch, Ellis Rabb was destined to return to the Wellesley campus to direct as well as perform for Group 20, and here he was to meet and later marry the present leading lady of the APA, Rosemary Harris.

In the meantime, however, from 1952 to 1957 Ellis Rabb returned to Antioch summer after summer, loyal to a program which eventually produced the entire canon of Shakespeare's works, including *The Two Noble Kinsmen.* He appeared in most of these productions, directed some of them, stretched himself, and grew as an actor in such diverse roles as the Duke of York in *Henry VI;* Old Gremio, Old Capulet, Bassanio, Justice Shallow, the Archbishop of Canterbury, and the Dauphin in *Henry V;* Benedick, Touchstone, Cassius, Troilus, King Lear, Leontes, Ariel, and Cardinal Wolsey. Of his performance of King Lear, Henry Hewes said, reviewing one of the later seasons in the *Saturday Review:*

> Ellis Rabb, who in the season of 1956 in New York received critical lines of praise longer than his part (Starveling in "Midsummer Night's Dream") jumps back to acting with a vengeance in the title role of "King Lear." The twenty-six-year-old actor shows us a Lear that, though it be something short of old age's pain and recalled experience, has all the technical finish, brilliance, and intelligence of a Sir John Gielgud.

What Rabb and all of his associates were finding in the Antioch years of Shakespearean repertory was that there were special challenges, problems, and values in repertory not available in isolated performances, whether long-run Broadway hits or one-week stands in summer stock. Several plays rehearsed early in a season and then played intermittently all season grew in a remarkable and unforeseeable way. Each time a play returned to the repertory after a week's layoff, new values were found, fresh meanings discovered, ensemble nuances of action and reaction developed, so that each season ended not with the familiar relief of summer stock but with the aesthetic regret of an inspiration not fully realized.

Not only in the playing, but in the very meanings of the plays were there found to be unexpected values. One play was sharpened in its relation to another. Comedy became more sharply pointed in repertory with tragedy, and tragedy more profound. Ellis Rabb and Barbara Waide, playing a hilarious Benedick and Beatrice in a Sunday matinee and a profound Lear and Regan the same evening to substantially the same audience, found for the first time an actor's satisfaction in repertory.

Ellis Rabb's associates in the Antioch Festival were eventually to form the main strength of the Association of Producing Artists, actors and actresses who became charter members of the organization—David Hooks, Nancy Marchand, Paul Sparer, Jacqueline Brooks, Clayton Corzatte, Tucker Ashworth, Joyce Ebert, Michael Ebert, and many others.

On New Year's Day 1960 Rabb invited to his apartment in New York a large group of acquaintances and friends with whom he had enjoyed professional association over the previous half-dozen years. They were actors, stage managers, designers, technicians, many of whom were familiar on the staffs of the Shakespeare Festival at Antioch, Group 20 at Wellesley, and an off-Broadway tradition at that time strongly classical in persuasion. It was his notion, as he outlined it to his friends, that the fate of the theater should reside in the hands of the artists—not the commercial investors in "show business."

It was his intention to put this notion into practice by forming an association of artists to work in this common cause. The logical name must be "the Association of Producing Artists." The acronym APA quickly followed. Heady plans were soon brewing, production possibilities came and went. A summer season in Bermuda had already been negotiated. Workshop groups were to be instituted immediately. A studio home had been found in a neighboring loft. APA was on its way.

In the meantime a study had been launched at Princeton University by a committee composed of members of the administration and the faculty to determine a proper disposition of the McCarter Theater, a large, comfortable, and generally well-appointed theater on the Princton campus.

The McCarter had been built in 1928 with funds supplied by the assets of the Princeton Triangle Club, a generous donation of alumnus Thomas N. McCarter, and the technical cooperation of the university. Over a period of nearly thirty years it had been pretty conclusively demonstrated that the facility was too large a responsibility for an undergraduate club devoted to one original revue each year and too valuable a property to be left to the vagaries of temporary lessees for professional or amateur bookings.

The McCarter Theater Committee, with the professional guidance of Milton Lyon, developed a plan for a guided expansion of the McCarter Theater's use to become Princeton's "Center for the Performing Arts." It happened that these plans matured at precisely the time that Ellis Rabb's Association of Producing Artists had come into existence. It was not long before Lyon and Rabb were holding conversations, the ultimate result of which was a producing cooperation for the fall and spring terms of 1960–1— "APA at McCarter."

The cooperation was in every way successful, except that both APA and its Princeton hosts had primary requirements in program planning. Neither organization was best served in accepting the program planning of the other, since each had different purposes to serve. It was successful enough that each organization served in its first year to define the feasibilities of the other's planning.

In the meantime, the University of Michigan, in setting up its Professional Program under the direction of Robert Schnitzer, had developed a diversified plan which offered more suitable circumstances of mutuality with APA's program planning. After the 1960–1 season at Princeton, APA entered into a three-year sponsored production series at the Lydia Mendelssohn Theatre on the Ann Arbor campus. The New York sponsorship of the Phoenix Theatre followed, and the results have been internationally publicized as the most successful of the various relationships between a university and a professional theater operation.

Princeton University, turning to its own resources as the responsible producers of professional offerings, has established its professional resident repertory company engaging performers for approximately twenty-six weeks each year in fall and spring seasons of continuous performance. The concept of the "living library of theater heritage" is made available to the university community, the general public, and school groups from the entire region.

A full student generation has now been given the opportunity to witness a wide range of performances. Since the season of APA, a series of titles grouped under general headings have included a season of Bernard Shaw and Thornton Wilder, Shakespeare's

Contemporaries, the Mediterranean Heritage, plays of personal ambition, the feminine temper, a Quadricentennial Shakespeare Festival, a retrospect of American plays, and European Comedy from Aristophanes to Pirandello.

Currently Princeton's McCarter Theater has entered into negotiations with the Great Lakes Shakespeare Association of the greater Cleveland, Ohio, area. Under plans now maturing, the Princeton group will be in practically continuous repertory the year-round at its home theater at the university or in a seasonal location elsewhere. As in the case of the Phoenix Theatre, the University of Michigan and APA, the McCarter company will be preparing offerings in one location which will serve an entirely different public in another area to the mutual artistic, economic, and educational benefit of all concerned.

In following generally the progress of APA and the McCarter Theater as professional developments originated in close cooperation with educational institutions I have mentioned, specifically Princeton, the University of Michigan, Antioch, and Wellesley. However, it is important to stress that colleges and universities almost too numerous to detail have been developing a variety of relationships with what is academically named "the professional arts community." An attempt at even a partial listing of plans sought or under development on American campuses would inevitably ignore significant and unique explorations. Apart from those programs which we may observe at firsthand, we must, in a general discussion, deal in generalities.

There are two professional organizations which have taken active steps toward specific cooperation with university plans in professional programming—the American National Theatre and Academy (ANTA) and the Actors' Equity Association. Chartered by Act of Congress in 1935, ANTA serves as a coordinating agency and membership organization of professional, amateur, academic, community, and civic theater groups. It performs services of consulting, publicity, information exchanges, and placement for all levels of personnel for member groups throughout the country. The great majority of organized theater operations on American campuses—undergraduate, graduate, and professional—are group members of ANTA.

One of the services for which ANTA has been noted since the inception of its activities has been its assistance to campus organizations in engaging established professional artists for featured appearances in campus dramatic offerings. Some of these artists are well-known stars who appear for relatively modest honoraria; some are lesser-known but skilled professionals, who have a special penchant as "artists in residence," performing informal instructional services in an active laboratory of theatrical performing art.

There is no accurate record of the number of instances where artists in residence have appeared in campus theatrical productions, but an Equity spokesman estimates "about 200." The pattern was established in informal arrangements in 1947, with what have been termed the "letter form of contract" between a professional individual and an educational or cultural institution. In a significant number of instances, performers were alumni of colleges making artistic contributions in recognition of their mentors.

Actors' Equity Association, one of the bargaining unions representing legitimate, musical, variety, and radio-television artists, regularized and recognized the "letter form of contract" in 1954, after it had been in informal use for some half-dozen years. Therefore the first such contract of professional record appears considerably later than its actual use. The first record at Equity is the contract with Frances Starr, who appeared in a production at the University of North Carolina in 1954.

Actors' Equity Association, however, has been able to proceed on a far wider front in developments on the American campus than has the American National Theater and Academy. The professional association is motivated by several factors: increased opportunities of employment for its membership, regularizing of conditions of employment, awareness of the increasing economic activities in the so-called "culture market," accomplished and in prospect, and a genuine interest in the academic community's getting off to the right start in its professional undertakings.

A couple of years ago, financed by the Equity Foundation, the Association appointed Milton Lyon, whose success at Princeton was a strong qualification, to undertake professional direction of a "department to extend professional Theater." A man of great energy and zeal, Milton Lyon has in a very short time seen and assisted in many accomplishments of professional theater arts on campuses. A conversation with Mr. Lyon develops a general profile of those developments.

"There are two styles of campus plans," says Mr. Lyon, "those where the professional unit has no connection at all with a teaching department and those where the theater personnel will also gain faculty status and serve as professional instructors. There are combinations of these factors, but all the programs are predominantly one or the other of these styles."

Mr. Lyon points to the Theater Group, performing under the Theater Extension Program of the University of California at Los Angeles, as an example of the first-named "style" of operation.

Here an independent organization, with its own financial and legal responsibility, leases various university auditoriums for its offerings, paying a specified rental, and connected with the university's operations only through the university's extension services. The university participates in no administrative planning or operation and acquires no liabilities of the operation. Neither may it make any demands of the Theater Group related to undergraduate or graduate instruction.

The other "style of operation," as Milton Lyon terms it, is characterized by developments at both Stanford University and Stephens College. On these campuses, plans are being worked out and regularized with Actors' Equity to retain professional performers as faculty appointments. Rather than engage the company on Equity contracts of limited duration, the plans at Stanford and Stephens would be to place them on yearly stipends as ancillary instructors in classrooms, creative workshops, and seminars.

An interesting sidelight on the policy problems as between a university and a professional organization may be seen in unsuccessful negotiations between Stanford and San Francisco's Actors' Workshop. With generous financial encouragement from the Ford Foundation, a plan was promulgated whereby the Workshop would serve as Stanford's professional resident theater. In a situation roughly similar to that between Princeton University and the Association of Producing Artists, however, the prerogatives of program planning of the academic community and that of the professional theater administration were deemed to be mutually exclusive, and the partnerships in both cases were unworkable. Princeton's solution of the problem was to become technically a theatrical producer with its own staff; Stanford's plan would seem to be to encourage performers to become professors.

Significantly, there is one unique plan in development distinct from the "styles" of operation mentioned by Milton Lyon on the already established campuses. Still largely on the drawing boards, but already in operation as a pilot plant, the University of California at San Diego already has its physical planning, its funds, its department heads, and its forward motion for a vast new program to be serving 27,500 students between 1985 and 1990. Twenty-seven thousand five hundred will be the enrollment at new campuses at Santa Cruz and Irvine and already existing branches at Los Angeles, Santa Barbara, and Berkeley. Dr. John L. Stewart, Assistant to the Chancellor for the Arts, describes his theater plans in a letter as follows:

We are just beginning to make our plans for the arts, and as yet we have neither a program nor a faculty in drama. We need both urgently, for we have before us not just the opportunity to make a fresh start in the challenging and controversial field of academic theater, but another almost as exciting. For in 1968, an internationally known theater director will come to La Jolla to establish a repertory company. He has agreed to spend forty weeks a year in La Jolla for at least three years to get things underway. We shall be working closely with him.

The theatre building he will use is to be erected on the edge of the UCSD campus and will be financed, if all goes as planned, by the university and a local foundation. The two will share the theater on a 50–50 basis. (There will, of course, be other theaters on the campus.) It is hoped that out of this co-operative enterprise between a professional company and a great new university will come drama of high excellence.

Such developments as these cause Mr. Lyon to say of the work of Equity's Department to Extend Professional Theater: "The chief area of growth and energy is the California coast, particularly the Los Angeles area."

Besides the campus professional programs already mentioned, how many plans, I asked Mr. Lyon, are in active development in mutual planning with the professional community? "About twenty," was Mr. Lyon's estimate. "Five or six of these plans are cooking with the active ingredients of a well-developed prospectus and substantial support in facilities and financing. There are at least seven which are cooking but have no accurate plan or recipe of ingredients. Half a dozen plans have as yet no ingredients, but are in the active talking stage."

Mr. Lyon sees the professional responsibility of getting the conversations started. His department at Equity offers free consulting services, it offers the outline of a feasible design for plans under varieties of campus circumstances, it recommends feasibilities, it helps find trained personnel both to activate studies or to set up administration, and serves further as an information center and exchange of ideas.

What general conclusions may the observer draw from the somewhat obscure picture of the current developments in relations between the American campus and the professional theater? It would appear that the state universities feel a first responsibility to departmental programs in theater instruction, but they would like to cooperate with established professional operations. The Ivy League colleges have taken significant steps in the current academic generation. Dartmouth has established a drama department recently and constructed a 17.5-million-dollar arts building known as Hopkins Center, with several auditoriums and a summertime professional resident program. Harvard seems contented with its very active undergraduate program, extracurricular in scope, at the handsome Loeb Center. Brown University would like to develop a cultural center but is limited by the considerations of the crowded Providence real estate picture. Princeton has become a theatrical producer with an expanding program at its McCarter Theater. The University of Pennsylvania is one of those programs which Mr. Lyon describes as cooking but with no active ingredients. Cornell has launched initial studies in program plans and is cooperating with a Festival Arts Association sponsored by public-spirited citizens of Ithaca. Yale has its Yale Drama School for professional training.

The smaller colleges are served mostly by ANTA's program of cooperation in providing visiting single luminaries; some activate their campus activities in the summertime with technical assistance to visiting groups, after the manner of Antioch, Williams, Wellesley, or Brandeis. And Stephens College, a women's campus in Columbia, Missouri, plans to name professional theater artists as teaching associates.

If I may hazard a personal opinion, there is one outstanding impression after twenty years of intimate association with campus professional theater operation. The campus movement toward professional arts seems to have the motivation of instinct rather than that of deliberative academic planning. It is quite clear that the campus planners are not professional theater people. Many planners have had only the most limited experience with the commitments required by professional programming, commitments which are complicated in areas of financial, legal, and administrative responsibilities as well as aesthetic, emotional, and intellectual ones.

Yet the plans go forward as if by some tacit assumption that the time has come when the centers of the humanities must assume a leadership in the best of our heritage. It would be sentimental to assume that this is a conditioned response to the ghastly aesthetics of the theater of the existential, the angry, and the absurd, and yet the sentiment is worth investigation. It would be irresponsible to assume that the universities can assume indefinitely the outsize financial liabilities of theatrical producing, and yet some responsible agency must prepare the staffs of the burgeoning cultural centers.

By and large, the American scheme of producing its theater has been hit or miss. Commercial considerations have far and away dominated any aesthetic ones, with the result that America's not inconsiderable contribution to the art of the theater has been the American musical comedy. However, it is plain as America prepares instinctively its own cultural coming of age that there is something missing. Missing are the traditional, well-established resident theaters in the manner of the European repertory theaters. Missing are the conservatories in association with such repertories. Missing, therefore, is professional training in a professional milieu, for all the excellence of theater departments of various universities.

It has not been the purpose of this article to elaborate the policy and administrative woes that have confronted the colleges and universities in their moves toward resident professional arts; needless to say, anxieties have been considerable.

The fact is, however, for richer or for poorer, in sickness and in health, the American campus and the American professional theater are taking vows of mutual assistance to bring into existence something as yet not clearly defined but thus far missing from the American cultural scene.

15 THE EDUCATIONAL THEATER IN AMERICA

Edwin Burr Pettet

While it is often difficult for American educators to agree on how the purposes of higher education in this country can be most fully realized, there is a satisfying high percentage of agreement among them on what those purposes are. Or to put it another way, a governing principle exists to which most of us subscribe even though we are never quite satisfied at any moment that we are putting that principle into effective practice. Our college curricula are constantly up for revision, in the shop for overhaul, so to say, under the supervision of the college or university educational policy committee, whose members, in their exasperating work, often spend as much time in committee meetings as they do in classrooms or in their individual research.

The central principle behind American higher education is unquestionably a difficult one to implement, if for no other reason than that the goal toward which that principle drives defies exact definition. Descriptions of the ideally educated man, the qualities he should possess, and the educational experiences and disciplines that will form him have a way of slipping into frustrating vagueness or embarrassing pieties. Yet somewhere in the first few pages of every American college or university catalogue you will find a statement setting forth in words the portrait of the wise and ethical man which the programs of study presented in the catalogue's subsequent pages are expected to bring to life. The catalogues speak of the man capable of making moral decisions, the well-rounded individual, the full-orbed personality. We use phrases like "solid background" and "historical perspective" and "breadth of vision" and "sensitivity to tradition"; and while such catalogue statements seem to have a greater knack of diluting intentions than of revealing them, there is somewhere within the pious phrases an instructional purpose, or perhaps it should be called a dream, to which the American educator is committed.

The liberal arts college, or more accurately the college of liberal arts and sciences, is the instrument of that commitment, and of the fifteen hundred institutions of higher learning in this country, the vast majority of them have since their inauguration been centered in that commitment.

Some of those institutions like Swarthmore, Oberlin, and Carleton are colleges of arts and sciences only. But even at great universities—Yale, Harvard, Princeton, and the massive state universities with their graduate and professional schools—you will always find a group of buildings that form the heartland of each, the college of arts and sciences, where for four years American students seek both breadth of understanding in human thought and affairs and depth in the area of their own specialty. It is this combination of breadth and depth that structures each student's program of study during his undergraduate years. If his field of specialization is, let us say, French philology and literature, he will expect to give approximately one third of his course and preparation time to that concentration. He will devote a second third of his time to university requirements, courses which for want of a better term are called "general education" or the "core curriculum." In this group he will be required to study a natural and a biological science, history, philosophy, English and American literature, and perhaps psychology or sociology. In the remaining third of his curriculum, he is free to elect courses at his own discretion. He may return to his specialization if he wishes or he may wander afield into courses in mathematics, art, music, or drama, or pursue in some depth a second field of interest. The structure varies of course from institution to institution, but the principle of specialization, then requirements, then electives is universal enough in American education to be called characteristic.

I am speaking generally about the philosophy of American education only because I feel that the present subject—the study of drama and theater in our colleges and universities—can be properly understood only when it is seen emerging from that philosophy and subsequently taking a legitimate place as a specialization in undergraduate studies. Briefly the story is this.

With the disappearance of the traveling theatrical companies after the turn of the present century, vast expanses of the United States were left barren of living drama. It was natural enough that college students with an inclination toward performing would gather into amateur societies and produce plays on the campuses for their own amusement and occasionally self-edification. Quite often the impulse to stage such plays had its origins in English literature classes, and it was not unusual for one or another of the English literature professors to try his hand at producing. By the middle of the 1930's almost every campus had such an amateur theater society, and while they frequently produced ordinary, warmed-over Broadway fare, it was not unheard of for work of a worthwhile experimental nature to be undertaken as well. Many small communities close to university campuses and some of considerable size throughout the country depended upon such college thespians for their entire theater experience. Broadway is a long distance from the cornfields of Iowa and the ranges of Texas.

When some of the leading large universities established full departments of speech correction during the mid-1930's, relieving English literature departments of their obligations to this expanding discipline, the fledgling drama societies were offered the administrative hospitality of speech departments. Of course the English literature departments held on to most of the courses in which the drama was treated as a literary study. Students concentrating in theater within speech departments were concerned primarily with performance: acting, stage design, and producing. For Shakespeare, Shaw, and the Continental playwrights, they went elsewhere in the university. It was scarcely a satisfactory arrangement. Theater is connected to the speech disciplines only by the thread of voice and diction studies and the tradition of declamation. It is wholly removed from speech departments' preoccupation with cleft palates, the lisp, and the stutter. Yet in order to enjoy some degree of administrative autonomy which speech departments offered them, theater teachers waived their claim to the literature of the drama, an exclusion that forced upon their discipline a lopsided structure.

Time, however, was to work a remedy. By the end of World War II, two tendencies were active. First, theater teachers argued their right to exist as a separate discipline, as a departmental specialty in undergraduate studies, won their case in numerous instances, and severed administrative connections with "speech." Second, as an effect of this independence, graduate departments of theater studies began to blossom all over the country in universities qualified to offer advanced degrees. With that accomplishment, the strongest note of educational respectability had been struck, and with the inauguration of graduate seminars in theater history, aesthetics, and dramatic literature as support to courses in the performance skills, little doubt remained in the minds of the philosophers of education that another discipline had emerged to legitimacy in graduate and undergraduate study. Presently more than four hundred colleges and universities confer the baccalaureate degree upon students with a concentration in the theater arts, one hundred eighty-five offer the advanced degrees of master of arts or doctor of philosophy in theater.

In those institutions where undergraduate departments of theater have secured the greatest administrative independence, courses and seminars now include a wide range of theater studies. There are always, of course, the training courses in performance skills: acting, producing, playwriting, scenic design, and dance. Indeed most undergraduate departments stress such creative studies. But within the past ten or fifteen years there has been an increasing number of courses in the literature of the drama within theater departments—courses in Greek and Roman drama, the Elizabethan, the seventeenth and the eighteenth centuries, modern, and contemporary; also courses in dramatic theory and criticism, in aesthetics, and in the history of theater architecture and styles. At the graduate level, the doctorate degree demands a concentration upon historical studies, dramatic criticism, and analysis. Students preparing for the master of fine arts degree usually concentrate in the performance arts: acting, scenic design, producing—or they may elect the increasingly important specialties of theater administration or technical production.

The scene is far from a static one. Indeed it is changing with astonishing rapidity. Each year more and more universities inaugurate graduate departments in theater studies. More undergraduate departments emerge each year and established ones expand. Students graduating with a bachelor's degree with a concentration in theater studies number in the thousands annually. Master's- and doctoral-degree recipients number in the high hundreds.

It would be very gratifying if I could say that this expansion of theater training within our centers of higher education was responsible for a glorious renaissance in American theater artistry. It would be a satisfying justification of money spent on campus theater buildings, of student and teacher energy, and of the philosophy of education that has generated collegiate theater studies, if I could document our achievements with a roster of brilliant college-trained actors, imaginative producers, and significant playwrights who are making an impact on international theater culture in anything approaching the force that our emphasis upon theater education would appear to warrant. There is much that is fresh and imaginative in the American professional theater, and I certainly do not intend to disparage it. But even if one could ascribe the success of our contribution in the international theater scene wholly to the educational theater—which I am sure we cannot—it would scarcely justify our system in the light of the European theater, which is not served as we are by the universities but by professional schools and academies. I have been privileged to examine closely the work done in a number of European theater schools, from the State Theater School in Warsaw to R.A.D.A. in London. I have also studied with great interest the operation of municipal and state repertory theaters on the Continent. As training centers for actors and producers, these professional schools are unquestionably superb. And for the encouragement of playwrights and of experimental movements in producing and designing, I can imagine nothing more invigorating than the European repertory system, with its permanent staff, its continuing management, and its resident dramaturgists and playwrights. This is the tradition of the Elizabethan theater, the Moscow Art Theatre, the Théâtre Libre, with what that tradition means in providing a context for the creative imagination. I am afraid that if we were to rest the case for the American university theater upon a comparison between its product and the product of the European system, it would take a very prejudiced judge to decide in our favor.

The case, however, does not rest there. Again let me say that I am not dismissing as insignificant the university's role in the training of professional theatrical artists. Quite a few of my own students have become highly successful as actors and producers. And some of the most important current producing talents—William Ball, Stuart Vaughn, William Penn, Work Baker—were trained within university theater departments. But the university theater is having an effect of far greater consequence than one that can be measured in numbers of highly skilled actors, playwrights, or technicians. Of first importance is this: it has built a massive and discerning audience for good theater ready from coast to coast to welcome the experimental and the classic. During his college years, the American student attends the campus theater productions as a pleasurable extension of his educational program. Whether he attends a university with a strong theater department, such as the Universities of Iowa and Illinois, or one with no official department at all, such as Harvard and Princeton, makes very little difference. He will see from two to ten productions in each of his four student years. And the plays he sees will range from last year's Broadway successes through the whole of the classic repertory to the contemporary experimental and avant-garde. With approximately six hundred thousand men and women completing their university education each year, there has been a vast population prepared for good theater during the past twenty years, prepared and ready to support it.

A second consequence of the growth of university theater departments is that they are becoming the headquarters for American theater scholarship and research. Thirty-five years ago our contribution to the International Theatre Institute could have been no more than a token one. Today American theater scholars, the greater number of whom are professors of drama and theater in university theater departments, are responsible for a growing body of significant books and papers on the theater's history, on theatrical producing, and theatrical criticism. It is ironic that the one theater periodical, *Theatre Arts Magazine,* that spoke for the professional theater should suspend publication at a time when university theater publications are on the increase. *Theatre Arts Magazine* is gone, its Broadway offices closed; but subsidized by universities or edited by university professors under foundation sponsorship are: *Drama Survey, The Tulane Drama Review, The Educational Theatre Journal, Players Magazine, Theatre Survey,* and others. As departments have grown, scholarship has increased, and in turn scholarship has enlightened the practice of theater everywhere, refined it of its crudeness, and given to its young artists not only knowledge and context but an ardent belief in the value of theater and a commitment to it as high art. We are witnessing at this moment in the United States the end of a long period in which both its audiences and its practitioners thought of the theater merely as show business. For this, the university is responsible.

Indeed what we are witnessing is both an end and a beginning, and while no single cause can account for so vast and complex a shifting of the American theater scene as I believe is taking place, it is undeniably true that without the existence of the university theater it could not have occurred. What is happening is this—the era of the stock company and the traveling road show, which once supplied a vast network of theaters and opera houses throughout the country, is gone beyond recall. Television and the motion picture have become the popular entertainment sources for countless millions of Americans who, because of the sheer size of this country, would expect perhaps only once in a lifetime to be able to visit New York and see a play. But what of New York? For a variety of reasons too numerous to detail here, the New York theater, both Broadway and off-Broadway, has been dwindling alarmingly in the past twenty-five years. To put it briefly: in a typical season in the 1930's, New York saw 233 productions. In the 1940 season, it saw 91. In 1960, there were a total of 58 plays presented. In 1963, the total was 54. In 1927, there were 77 Broadway theaters in operation; today there are 32.

But even as we watched with despair the shrinkage in New York we became aware that a more robust and vigorous and massive theater movement was evolving throughout the land centered in the universities, a direct consequence of the growth of theater departments, yet ironically neither intended nor foreseen by the professors and administrators, the scholars and artists, who had committed their careers to theater within the walls of Academia. And yet, was it not obvious? The universities had been training students in ever-increasing numbers for a professional theater industry that was slowly diminishing in importance and influence, an industry in which only the smash hit had any chance of survival. And to train the artists for such an industry, the universities had built beautiful and well-equipped theaters— many of them better equipped than any theater on Broadway. They built better than they knew, and better in more than one sense. Take the students who graduate from colleges or universities with a concentration in theater. Ten or twenty years ago there was only Broadway to beckon to them. Today they start in one of the numerous university summer theaters, the festival theaters that have mushroomed from Minnesota to Texas, from Oregon to Florida. Then they may return to the university as graduate students or artists-in-residence or they find engagements in the numerous municipal or community professional theaters, such as the Charles Playhouse in Boston, the Actors Workshop in San Francisco, the Alley Theatre in Houston, the Arena Stage in Washington, and dozens of other similar institutions, most of which were founded by young idealists trained in university theaters. Or the graduating student may be called to one of the four thousand amateur community-theater societies who want the services of a full-time, well-trained producer or technical director. Actors who once knew only New York now may never see New York, and young, experimental playwrights whose manuscripts accumulated on the desks of New York producers now send their plays to theater departments or work their plays through production while they serve as artists-in-residence on university campuses. Some graduates become secondary-school teachers of drama or producers of theater for children. Others work at "creative dramatics," as it is called—the staging of plays by young people as an exercise in imaginative self-expression. Students who have obtained advanced degrees—a master of arts or a doctor of philosophy—generally return to the university as professors of drama, scholars, and producers.

I don't mean to suggest that Broadway, Hollywood, and the television centers have suddenly lost their appeal. That, I am sure, they will never do. Students trained in universities or in our professional theater schools, such as the American Academy of Dramatic Arts, the Neighborhood Playhouse, and the Goodman Theatre will test their talents in these arenas as long as they exist. But already nearly as many actors, producers, and designers are gainfully employed in university-sponsored theaters as earn their livings performing plays in New York where the small-cast play has for financial reasons become the common type. It may be of interest to know that fourteen of a recent Broadway crop of plays, calling for two, three, four, and five characters each, employed a total of only forty-seven actors. So it is not surprising that the movement should be away from New York, back to the vast areas where audiences are waiting and university theater buildings are springing up to accommodate them. The United States has never enjoyed the tradition of state-subsidized theater and it is unlikely that any proposal for governmental financing of the theater would excite enthusiasm among our citizens. But unless I am wholly mistaken, there will be in this country within the next ten or fifteen years our own version of a subsidized theater centered in the university and paid for out of university funds, a theater reaching a far larger audience than the two million who buy tickets in New York each season and one far more imaginative and experimental than the hard-dollar practices of the New York theater can afford.

The campus theater is first of all a training laboratory, but it is also a community theater center and a library of living plays. And it is an astonishing fact that the university theater is witnessed by almost three times the number of people each year as attend the professional theater in New York. This is just the university theater; I am not including audiences of the professional community theaters or of the amateur theater societies. But if we look at the production ratio between the New York theater and the university theater, we find an even more astonishing comparison. Broadway produces approximately sixty plays in a year; the university theater presents twelve hundred productions a year, twenty times the number of the Broadway offerings. Furthermore, the university theater is host to visiting companies of actors, dancers, ethnic performers from Europe and Asia, as well as to concert theater productions which are especially designed to perform the university circuit.

We are witnessing only a beginning, as I noted before. We are in a time of promise rather than fulfillment, but the handwriting is apparent on the wall. It all began with a disturbing question— Should not potential artists of the theater be privileged to pursue their speciality within the structures of higher education, just as potential doctors, lawyers, economists, sociologists, schoolteachers, and engineers have long been privileged to do? The answer it appears is Yes.

Epilogue

16 THE FUTURE OF THE AMERICAN THEATER

Alan S. Downer

In the fall of 1965, the Yale University School of the Drama celebrated its fortieth anniversary by assembling a group of speakers
to talk about the future of the theater in America. Ultimately, I
suppose, it is foolish to try to predict the future of an art which is
above all others responsible to the society and culture which it
reflects without having a clear picture of what the future shape
of the society will be. The Yale speakers took refuge in imagination and in highly subjective wishful thinking; turning despair-
ing eyes from the moribund repertory of Broadway, they foresaw
new forms of playwriting, new freedom in theatrical architecture
and production, floods of public money for the support of new
enterprises. They were by turns wild, witty, and willful and, for
citizens of a nation commonly supposed to be practical, materialistic, pragmatic, they were as idealistic as the dwellers in a Utopia
of aesthetes. They did not so much predict as assert, and perhaps
that is as good a way to handle the future as any other.

There is, of course, another way to look into the future, and
since it is less imaginative, its vision is less revolutionary. However, it derives from a balanced view of the present and a careful
review of the past, so it will not be without value in concluding
this collection of articles on the Theater in American Life.

I do not believe that any of the previous writers has pretended
that the present state of the professional theater in America is
healthy. Centered on a few acres of fantastically expensive real
estate in New York, forced to tailor its offerings to the limited

tastes of hit-oriented customers, competing with the free and readily available pastime of television, it is surprising that the theater survives at all, or that it finds creative talents—writers, actors, directors, designers—who are willing to gamble their own lives on its survival. But this is perhaps the first fact on which to base a confident prediction that the American theater has a future. Theater people are not indifferent, of course, to the benefits of contemporary American society—education, social mobility, increased leisuretime for the pursuit of personal interests—and to achieve these benefits they must comply with the commercial demands of their profession, must work out their hours before cameras or in TV studios, or give something like human substance to the lightminded mechanical entertainments of Broadway. But regardless of the demands of commerce, they also give themselves willingly to the fuller practice of their art, working at a subsistence level off-Broadway or in the new repertory theaters mushrooming throughout the country. The theater will survive and expand because it alone can satisfy an urge peculiar and common to actors and playwrights: the need for a sustained experience created nightly in the presence of and responding to the reactions of a live audience.

Although the movies (and television plays, which are now almost entirely canned, like movies, for broadcast) have developed mechanical devices like the close-up for increasing their affective power, they are only a substitute for the full experience of drama. The theater is a living art—the playwright or director manipulates bodies and voices in actual time and visible space, creating afresh at each performance a unique total work of art, in which creation (to use the fine French term) the audience *assists*. The theater is a communal art: it is an experience shared by its performers (its company) and by its spectators—not by ones and twos in the living room but by hundreds in its special home, the playhouse. And this is the second fact on which to base a confident prediction that the American theater has a future—there is no equivalent, from the spectator's point of view, for the experience of living drama in a playhouse.

To test the validity of such a statement one has only to follow the reaction of what might be called the "junior audience," the adolescents who have been raised on movies and television, who find themselves, for the first time in their lives, members of the audience at the new local repertory theater. At first their behavior is completely unsophisticated, they talk to one another as they do during the commercials on TV, they make occasional forays into the lobby in search of popcorn or candy. But by their second visit they are beginning to respond to the human presences on the stage, they begin to sense the new order of reality unfolding on the stage. Standing at the back of the auditorium one can almost —despite the normal restlessness of youth—*feel* their engagement, feel their young minds and uncorrupted emotions being drawn into and responding to the life of the play. To some observers, the fervor of their response may seem naïve—I have heard them cry out as Romeo prepared for suicide or delay the final curtain of *A Midsummer Night's Dream* for a quarter of an hour by their uncontrollable laughter at the farce of Pyramus and Thisbe. Naïve or not, this unlocking of the power of emotional response is one of the purposes and rewards of playgoing, and a continuing compensation for the growing reticence of maturity. The ability to suspend disbelief willingly in the presence of art is a characteristic of a rich and humane, a genuinely affluent society.

Granted then that the theater must survive into the future because it is necessary to its artists and its audience, what kind of theater will it be?

As we venture into the ultimately unknowable, it will be well briefly to re-examine what kind of theater it has been, so that we may have at least a firm launching pad. From its beginning American drama has in its content and its attitudes been a popular art, reflecting the nation and its experience. *The Contrast*, often cited as the first completely American play, is a plea for recognition of native virtues and homespun wisdom as opposed to imitation of the artifices of European civilizations. The highly colored melodramatic repertory, which was the staple fare of the nineteenth-century stage, stresses those characters and situations which were the inevitable preoccupations of the audience outside the theater: the frontiersman and "manifest destiny," the Yankee and "self-reliance," the farmer and the immigrant and the problems of increasing urbanization, the Negro slave and the threat to national unity, commerce and industry and the threat to national innocence. And when melodrama gave way before the pressures of the new theater movement after World War I, the treatment may have changed but the subjects remained the same.

As a test, you have only to consider the plays of Eugene O'Neill, the leader and the outstanding product of the reformation. His early short plays about the life of the sailor are full of nostalgia for the farm, a kind of Eden; they uphold the dignity and importance of the individual whatever his status. In *The Emperor Jones* and *All God's Chillun Got Wings,* he writes of slavery and its consequences. *Beyond the Horizon* and *Desire Under the Elms* are concerned in part with the pioneer and the farm. The immigrant confronting an established society is the central figure of *A Touch of the Poet.* The materialism of American life is the subject of *Marco Millions.* Indeed O'Neill's final effort as a playwright was a projected nine-play cycle tracing the history of a representative American family from the Revolution of 1776 through the Great Depression of the 1930's. Aware that his time was running out, O'Neill attempted to destroy the drafts of his cycle, but the two plays that remain—*A Touch of the Poet* and *More Stately Mansions*—clearly indicate that the combination of themes—idealism versus materialism, human rights versus property rights, individual liberty versus social tyranny—and the selection of characters—farmer, sailor, immigrant, man of business—the combination that had always distinguished American drama, was a continuing concern even into the 1940's.

These themes did not lose their power after World War II. In *The Crucible,* Arthur Miller is still exploring the problem of balancing the rights of the individual against the necessities of a social organization; *Death of a Salesman* is in part a requiem for the pioneer trapped by urbanization. In *A Streetcar Named De-*

sire, Tennessee Williams writes of the renewal of expansionism and social mobility through the continuing flow of immigrants from the Old World, overwhelming and replacing values and attitudes that have become unrealistic or outmoded. The comic spirit, always an expression of the national optimism, continues to dominate the works of Murray Schisgal, William Hanley, and other writers of the present-day avant-garde. As the repertory of American drama continues to grow, it reasserts the subject matter and, with varying emphases, the attitudes with which the life of the stage has for two centuries reflected the life of the audience.

But if the American dramatic repertory has in its subjects and attitudes reflected the essential concerns of the breadth and depth of the American audience, it has reflected in its forms and techniques American culture in quite a different way. One must constantly be reminded that the only native Americans are Indians, that the United States is a society of immigrants. Some of the men who signed the Declaration of Independence from Great Britain had been on this continent only a few years, none were of families that had been here more than a few generations. From the beginning of the nineteenth century the nation replenished its human resources from waves of immigrants. The immigrant enriched and expanded both the nation and its drama, for the American theater has welcomed and absorbed continental dramatic forms as eagerly as the society welcomed and absorbed the English, the Germans, the Irish, the Scandinavians, the Italians, and the Central Europeans who came to these shores.

Our earliest plays imitated the forms current in the English theater of the eighteenth century: comedy of manners, debased Elizabethan blank-verse tragedy, ballad opera. The romantic movement reached us through translations and adaptations of the German Kotzebue. The panoramic form of melodrama with its realistic settings, spectacular actions, and domestic entanglements came first from France with not-inconsiderable additions from England. From France, too, came the well-made play and the *drame-à-thèse* of the mid-nineteenth century, plays written under the aegis of Eugene Scribe and Dumas *fils.* Ibsen found a ready welcome as dramaturge, though his "problems" seemed something less than radical to a society that had been founded on a break with the traditions of the past. The iconoclasm of Bernard Shaw found a readier audience in New York than in London, and touring companies from Dublin's Abbey Theatre inspired the development of an American folk drama. The influence of the Swedish August Strindberg on O'Neill is well known; it should be further recognized that Strindberg's spareness, violence, and freedom of form found a ready response in American playwrights generally—he has probably been the greatest single influence on modern American drama. With the 1920's, as America became more and more politically and commercially involved with the transatlantic world, the theater exposed its audiences to the widest range of foreign influences. Individual producers, and organizations such as the Theatre Guild, actively sought out new dramatists and new dramatic forms; Luigi Pirandello, Georg Kaiser, and Jean Giraudoux were welcomed and absorbed into the mainstream. More recently, of course, such playwrights as Samuel Beckett, Eugene Ionesco, Harold Pinter, and—above all —Jean Genet have sent us their offspring and have found enthusiastic acceptance, particularly among the younger generation of playwrights and playgoers.

Such plays and playwrights, however, are important not merely for broadening or internationalizing the American repertory but because they have been absorbed into the experience of American playwrights. Earlier in this volume Edward Albee and Murray Schisgal both acknowledged a debt to Jean Genet, yet none of their plays is an imitation of Genet. The flatness, the marvelous ear for colloquial speech, the sense of menace which are the qualities of Harold Pinter may underlie the dramaturgy of Jack Richardson, but *Gallows Humor* is distinctively his own, and American. Beckett's black allegories of emptiness and despair have played in every city and college theater in the country, but American playwrights have responded by creating grotesque allegories whose comic vitality mocks the emptiness of their characters' attitudes.

The analogy between theater and society is thus an exact one: each wave of immigration brought new qualities and a renewed vitality to the nation, and was ultimately absorbed in the cultural stream; each dramaturgical influence brought new techniques to the drama and was ultimately absorbed in the native repertoire.

One of the consequences of the absorption of foreign (particularly European) influences was that American plays became more and more exportable. A century ago an English critic might rhetorically ask, Who reads an American book or goes to an American play?—without sounding more than ordinarily supercilious. But, as far as the drama was concerned, an answer began to become possible with the award of the Nobel Prize for Literature to Eugene O'Neill. Thornton Wilder's *Our Town* found a worldwide audience, demonstrating that although it was as American in substance as blueberry pie, its dramaturgy permitted it to speak to all cultures in familiar and touching ways. And the playwrights who came to Broadway after World War II—most prominently Williams and Miller—met equally receptive hearing far from New York. This ready interchange of dramatic experiences is not an American phenomenon, of course, but the distinguishing characteristic of the modern theater. Twenty years ago, Armand Salacrou, the French playwright, observed that "the dramatic author has been liberated. . . . He is no longer the prisoner of a narrow circle to whose rules he must submit or remain silent. He need no longer woo the public on the little island where his birth placed him during his passage through life. . . . There are hundreds of other small islands available for conquest."

This is not to say that anything goes, anywhere. Arthur Miller's *Death of a Salesman,* perhaps the serious play most successful with American audiences in recent decades, was equally successful in Germany, but was a failure in England. His drama of Salem witchcraft, *The Crucible,* was a comparative failure on its first production in New York, was widely successful in Scandinavia, was made into a fascinating film in Paris, and then was revived for a two-year run in New York. Here, I think, we must recognize how deeply social conditions can influence the success or failure of a production. The essential drama of *The Crucible* was obscured in its original production by its apparent reference to a contemporary political controversy in Washington. In Scandinavian countries the true theme of the play was strengthened by audiences' awareness of their own past, the more universal implications of a reign of Unreason represented by the persecution of so-called witches, implications which had already been made impressive by *Day of Wrath,* the classic Danish film by Carl Dreyer. When the play returned to New York, the contemporary controversy had been stilled and the true meaning of the play presented itself directly and impressively to the American audience.

Conversely, not every successful European playwright has found an equal welcome in the American professional theater. Two playwrights of wide continental repute, though of very different character, have had a peculiar history.

Earlier, both Mr. Albee and Mr. Schisgal as playwrights paid tribute to Bertolt Brecht, and there is no question that he has been a strong influence on the younger generation of American dramatists and—in particular—on the younger generation of American playgoers in the college and university theaters. But his only substantial success in the professional theater was *The Threepenny Opera* in a revised, Americanized version. Even such a masterpiece as *Mother Courage* found no welcome. His rejection is not a matter of politics, because every shade of political position has been represented in the professional theater of our day. Nor was it a matter of content: American audiences have been receptive to attacks on war, on tyranny, injustice, and they have accepted plays about gangsterism as metaphors for the evils of the system of free enterprise; and even in the adulterated *Threepenny Opera* they showed their willingness to accept the irony of vice and inhumanity encased in the conventions of popular music. The reasons for a particular failure are of course always multiple—casting, directorial error, and timing all may enter in. But the reason for consistent failure cannot lie simply in the accidents of occasion.

Jean Anouilh presents a similar problem. Perhaps half of his enormous output has been transported to New York and every combination of production circumstances has been attempted to gain a favorable hearing. Special casts of the principal and most popular American actors have been assembled (Helen Hayes and Susan Strasberg for *Mlle. Colombe*); highly successful London productions have been imported intact (*The Rehearsal*); a combination of English and American stars has been tried (Laurence Olivier and Anthony Quinn in *Becket*). But Anouilh's one success in New York was *L'Alouette* (*The Lark*) radically adapted by Lillian Hellman and starring Julie Harris, a young actress with a wide following. Again, it is not a matter of politics or of social attitude, for Anouilh's view of society and human nature is surely no blacker than O'Neill's. Nor does the American audience reject his subject matter as "too historical"—St. Joan, after all, has long been a popular figure, and T. S. Eliot's play about Becket has held the stage for many years. And, as in the case of Brecht, if mistakes have been made in the casting or interpretation of individual plays, the failure is too consistent to be charged to such particulars.

No, different though they may be in dramaturgy and philosophy, Brecht and Anouilh share a characteristic which the American audience seems unready to accept. They repeatedly draw back from their work, they interrupt the dramatic experience—in the case of Brecht to comment on it, in the case of Anouilh to mock its validity. And this brings us to a final point about the nature of the American theater and its probable future. It is, and presumably will remain, a theater of commitment, not a commitment to a particular social code or complex of ideas, for these have changed in the past and will continue to change. I mean simply a commitment to the idea of drama, that it is experience, serious experience, that it is a surrender of your own life for several hours to the life of the play.

Again there is the danger that this may sound naïve. One remembers the story of the gold miner who was driven by the "cunning of the scene" to draw his pistol and shoot the actor who was about to make mincemeat of the hero. Or, more recently, the lady who rose from her seat in the orchestra, walked onstage, and slapped the face of the leading player of *Look Back in Anger.* Commitment to the dramatic experience begins with this childish unwillingness to distinguish the play from reality, but it has deeper implications.

In America, as previous writers have suggested, playgoing is not easy. It involves booking seats sometimes three, sometimes six months in advance. It involves the expenditure of a considerable sum of money—for tickets, for transportation, for other expenses incidental to a full evening in a metropolitan setting. Many spectators fly several thousand miles for a week of playgoing; special trains and buses are rented for theater trips. Playgoing is not occasional, it is an occasion. It cannot be lightly undertaken; it cannot be lightly experienced.

Is it paradoxical that an audience that finds playgoing a serious business should patronize musicals and light comedies, should demonstrate "bad taste" in the selection of its dramatic experiences? Paradoxes are often more apparent than real, and the matter of bad taste may be subject to a little examination. To be sure, the best musicals cannot contest for the bays with *Hamlet,* the most skillful sex comedies do not threaten the stature of Molière. And neither will form a permanent part of the literature of the theater.

But the literature of the theater, the permanent shelf of dramatic classics, has always been much smaller than the *repertory* of the theater, the plays which draw and hold audiences night after night. It is not just in America that audiences are drawn more to performances than to play texts; it is the player who attracts our first allegiance. And it is certainly true that in recent decades those American players who have been most attractive—the most enfolding personalities, the most skilled craftsmen—have found their vehicles in the musical play and comedies of sex and domesticity.

However, it should be emphasized that musicals and light comedies can fail disastrously and that serious plays are not automatically doomed to indifference. As these words are written the outstanding success of this past Broadway season—the hot ticket, as they call it—was a play written by a German living in Sweden and performed by the Royal Shakespeare Company of London. Its abbreviated title was *Marat/Sade,* the setting was a French madhouse in the eighteenth century, the characters were nearly all madmen, and the historical situation on which it is based was quite unknown to the general audience. Yet, even during the transportation strike that paralyzed the city of New York, *Marat/Sade* played nightly to standing room only. The performance was not, if the term may be pardoned, a *succès-fou;* it was not presented as a freak show, or "fun in a madhouse." It was by turns revolting and grotesque, there were moments when you wanted to look away from the horror on the stage; and it was interpenetrated with discussions totally inconclusive and totally lacking in Shavian forensics. But from beginning to end, *Marat/Sade* was experience; for two hours the audience shared another life the pertinence of which to their own lives was never in question. It was a performance they chose freely to attend, an experience they chose to subject themselves to, just as they may have chosen on previous evenings to attend the latest musical or *The Odd Couple.*

The American theater is eclectic, its matter and techniques come to it from the wide, wide world, and the American audience chooses commitment in its playwrights, its actors, and itself. That has been its history since World War I, and that, one supposes, will be its foreseeable future.

Index

DATE DUE
REMINDER

**Please do not remove
this date due slip.**